MORE PRAISE FOR
SPIRITUAL MENTORING: A

"*Spiritual Mentoring*, a worthy successor to Judy Harrow's first book, *Wicca Covens*, continues to teach us what religion — and being religious — really means. Here is a splendid source of ideas, observations, and references to cutting-edge literature for leader who wish to develop the advanced spiritual skills needed to guide people who seek a stronger and deeper religious experience on the Pagan path."

— Fritz Muntean, editor of *The Pomegranate*

"How do those with the rich knowledge and wisdom of their own spiritual experience pass this on to those just embarking on their spiritual journey? This book is a wonderful companion and resource for those desiring to be of service with integrity and maturity. Judy offers Pagan mentors an opportunity for insight into their own inner process in this mentoring role while deepening their work with others."

— Selene Vega, M.A., LMFT, psychotherapist, former editor of the Spiritual Emergence Network Newsletter, and coauthor with Anodea Judith of *The Sevenfold Journey*.

"As a priestess, Judy Harrow examines, weighs, tastes, blends, and stirs a potent brew. Using inclusive language and respecting all our intertwining and diverging Pagan paths, the author adds depth, breadth, and maturity to our Pagan faith traditions, and she does it with erudition and grace."

— M. Macha NightMare, P&W, author of *Witchcraft and the Web: Weaving Pagan Traditions Online* and co-author of *The Pagan Book of Living and Dying*.

Spiritual Mentoring

A PAGAN GUIDE

Spiritual Mentoring
A PAGAN GUIDE

JUDY HARROW

ECW PRESS

Published by ECW PRESS
2120 Queen Street East, Suite 200, Toronto, Ontario, Canada M4E 1E2

NATIONAL LIBRARY OF CANADA CATALOGUING IN PUBLICATION DATA

Harrow, Judy
Spiritual mentoring: a pagan guide / Judy Harrow.
ISBN 1-55022-519-7
1. Spiritual life—Paganism. 1. Title.
BF1571.H36 2002   299   C2002-902197-9

Acquisition Editor: Emma McKay
Editor: Jodi Lewchuk
Typesetting: Wiesia Kolasinska
Production: Heather Bean
Printing: Webcom
Cover and interior design: Guylaine Régimbald—Solo Design
Front cover image: *The Blush*, by Eleanor Fortescue Brickdale
Reprinted courtesy Sotheby's Picture Library.

This book is set in Fairfield, Bickham Script, and Waters Titling

The publication of *Spiritual Mentoring: A Pagan Guide* has been generously
supported by the Government of Canada through the Book
Publishing Industry Development Program   Canadä

DISTRIBUTION

CANADA: Jaguar Book Group, 100 Armstrong Avenue,
Georgetown, Ontario L7G 5S4

UNITED STATES: Independent Publishers Group, 814 North Franklin Street,
Chicago, Illinois 60610

EUROPE: Turnaround Publisher Services, Unit 3, Olympia Trading Estate,
Coburg Road, Wood Green, London N2Z 6T2

AUSTRALIA AND NEW ZEALAND: Wakefield Press, 17 Rundle Street (Box 2066),
Kent Town, South Australia 5071

PRINTED AND BOUND IN CANADA

ECW PRESS
ecwpress.com

DEDICATION

The late Marjorie Nelson Brambir was a professional counselor and co-creator of the Counseling Basics for Priest/esses workshop, one of the antecedents of this book. The workbook that Margie and I created for those workshops eventually developed into the Counseling Basics Web site, <www.draknet.com/proteus/counselbook.html>. That's her gift to you, which I am proud to pass along.

Margie was also a beloved priestess, wife and mother, and a dear friend. Her sudden and tragic death left many of us shocked and too stunned even to conduct a memorial rite. This book was to be her memorial, till newer and harsher tragedy got in the way of it.

In her younger years, Margie worked as an Emergency Medical Technician. So in Margie's honor and on Margie's behalf, I dedicate this book to the EMTs and to all the people who died trying to save others at the World Trade Center.

CONTENTS

ACKNOWLEDGMENTS

Thanks and praise to all who have been mentors to me.

Thanks to the late Rev. Henry Brockmann, campus minister at Western College for Women during my undergraduate years there, who opened for me the whole area of contemporary theology.

Thanks to Margot. The more I learn about the might-have-beens, the more grateful I become for what actually was.

Thanks to Peter Bishop, Cat Chapin-Bishop, Barbara Glass, and Leon Reed for interviews I taped but never transcribed. Although your specific words are not in this book, your ideas are here. The stimulation I received from your conversation was immensely helpful.

Thanks to Moose, who knows why. Thanks to Maury and Vivian for a rescue I will never forget. Eternal thanks to Little Judy for a cup of coffee on Fordham Road.

Thanks to the people of Proteus, and thanks to the Internet for helping us stay connected despite separations of miles and years.

Thanks to the current Proteus puppy pile — to Ali, Donna, Elizabeth, Katie, Lynne, Maria, Rebecca, and Trent — for the pleasure of your company.

Thanks, big-time, to Renee, coven maiden extraordinaire.

Thanks to Brian and Gwyneth, my lifemates.

Thanks to Jennie Dunham, my agent, who always pushes the agenda.

Thanks to Emma McKay, my editor, for being there, accessible and understanding.

Most of all, thanks to the Ancient Gods, who surprise us constantly. May this work and the manner of its sharing bring harm to none, good to many, and honor to You. So mote it be.

INTRODUCTION

This book is about relationship: relationship with the Ancient Gods and how it may be nurtured by relationship with an experienced elder, a mentor.

In Greek myth, the Goddess Athena assumed the form of Odysseus's counselor, Mentor, in order to guide and protect the young Telemachus in his father's absence. In time, the word *mentor* came into the English language, meaning a wise and trusted elder counselor or teacher. Mentors abound in the secular world of work. These elder colleagues help beginners sharpen their skills, develop working relationships, build a good reputation, and learn the "culture," the interpersonal style of any particular workplace and of the occupation in general.

A spiritual mentor helps people with their spiritual growth. Spiritual growth is the process of establishing, deepening, clarifying, and sustaining conscious contact with Deity, and using what we learn from that contact to illuminate and guide our daily lives. For most of us, spiritual growth involves finding or creating a community of like-minded people, a source of mutual nurturance and support. The collective experience of that community, gathered into a body of lore and a system of ritual and spiritual practice, is another resource for the spiritual growth of each member. Deity, community, and lore — a detailed exploration of our relationships with these three will be the core of this book.

I am a Pagan, a Wiccan, and a Priestess. You'll be reading a lot more about what those words mean throughout this book. For now, let's just say that they identify my own understanding of Deity; my religious community; and the symbols, stories, and practices that shape my understanding and my life. They are the context for my own experiences of being mentored and mentoring others. I can only write with confidence and knowledge about spiritual mentoring in the contemporary Pagan Traditions.

Notice that I've used the plural form: *Traditions*. Neo-Paganism is the loving reconstruction and adaptation of the indigenous religions of Europe. There have always been more than one, and there still are, although we hold certain basics in common. We are Asatruar, Druid, Wiccan, and more. We are finding our own religion, reassembling it, updating it, building replacement parts as we go along. I hope this book contributes to that effort.

To guide others in their spiritual quest is an awesome responsibility. No one who takes it casually should be doing it at all. In fact, it's not even the kind of career that young people consciously choose and systematically prepare for. Still, people have instinctive reactions to one another. They can tell whose example they would like to follow, whose insights might be helpful — perhaps yours. Their requests for your advice are a kind of external call to assume the mentor's role, a call from the community. If your heart responds to their need, that's a call from within, a call from the Gods. Following such a call is risky, but to ignore it is riskier still — for by following our authentic callings, each of us finds our bliss.

If you are hearing or following such a call, my heartfelt hope is that this book will give you a framework for understanding what you do as a mentor and some helpful techniques you can use in this work.

A mentor is a role model, a lore giver, a listener, a supporter, and a challenger. A mentor is sometimes a gatekeeper, an evaluator, and a dispenser of constructive criticism. But a Pagan mentor is never any sort of boss, which is why I am not using the more familiar term, *spiritual director*. In the Pagan spiritual traditions, direction always comes from within. The only proper role of the mentor is to help each seeker hear that inner voice more clearly and live their life in increasing congruence with what they hear.

Pagan mentors are not directors or supervisors. We are consultants, resource persons. The seeker sets the goals in response to their own needs, their own inner calls. Mentors provide the perspective of long experience and study, help seekers understand obstacles, and make suggestions for further progress. It's up to the seeker to consider those suggestions and act on them or not, always learning from the outcomes of those choices. Seekers may work with the same mentor for years, choose to change mentors, or even go it alone for a while.

You'll find that many faith traditions use the same metaphor for spiritual growth: a path. A path is a known developmental sequence that leads to enlightenment, or sanctification, or whatever a specific faith group takes as its goal.

If spirituality is a path, then the mentor is a guide, somebody who has walked that particular path before. Guides may not know as much about the countryside as trained agronomists or geologists would. Still, a guide can advise travelers about what to pack; warn them about speed traps or confusing intersections; show them the landmarks and pitfalls; tell them about side trips worth taking, good restaurants, inexpensive motels, and the best bookstores along the way. Travel is easier, better, maybe even safer, with an experienced traveling companion.

My religion, neo-Paganism, can be understood as a cluster of adjacent paths winding through a green forest, sometimes inter-twining — even combining for a stretch — and sometimes separating. My personal path is Wicca, which I understand to be a committed and intense form of Pagan service and practice. I expect that what I write will be most relevant to those who follow one of the Pagan paths. But I'm hoping others will find this book useful as well.

In preparing to write this book, I read a great deal of Christian writing about spiritual direction. Some of it seemed applicable, most did not. The process of figuring out what was and was not applicable and why really helped me focus on what is congruent and effective spiritual mentoring for us. Non-Pagans may find a Pagan book on mentoring gives them a similar stimulus. At the least, this book can offer them deeper insight into what Pagans do.

Some Pagan friends who read early drafts asked me why I drew so much on non-Pagan theorists and so little on traditional materials. The reason is that this book is written primarily for Pagan elders, people who are presumably already familiar with our heritage of traditional lore. My purpose is to introduce some new conceptual tools that I hope will be useful and to show you how they might supplement our ways of thinking about the process of spiritual development.

It's customary in an introduction to give a brief overview of the book. Here's mine:

CHAPTER 1
A Path of our Own: What Makes Paganism Different
Discusses the differences in our basic theology that lead
to some different approaches to spiritual development.

CHAPTER 2
Traveling Companions: Mentor and Student
Covers the issues of screening and matching mentors and
students.

CHAPTER 3
Safe Space: Nurturing Interactions
Discusses the relationship between mentor and student
and the interpersonal skills required for mentoring.

Chapter 4

Road Maps: Models of Maturity
Presents several theories of adult development, both
general and religious.

Chapter 5

Deity: Seeking Closeness
Discusses how the mentor can help the student develop a
relationship with the Ancient Gods.

Chapter 6

Community: Sharing Support
Discusses how the mentor can help the student find a
place in the Pagan community.

Chapter 7

Lore: Sharing Knowledge
Discusses how the mentor can help the student connect
with intellectual and spiritual ancestors, both meditatively
and through the cumulative legacy of myth and other lore.

That's one possible route through the book. In reality, there's no
compelling reason for this order. This material is neither linear
nor sequential. Each chapter is best understood in the light of
several of the other chapters. Please read the chapters in the
order of your own interest or need, and revisit them occasionally.
Or skip around. I've included lots of cross-referencing and two
alternative navigational aids.

First, I want to present the chapters in another familiar
format:
WHO: Chapter 2
WHAT: Chapters 5, 6, and 7

WHERE: Anywhere
WHEN: Chapter 4
WHY: Chapter 1
HOW: Chapter 3

Second, I've included an extensive and elaborate glossary. Like most authors, I've tried to define every word that might be new to some readers the first time I use it. The glossary is for people who are reading chapters in the order of their own interest or need, and therefore might miss the first appearance of a word. I'm also including page references with each glossary entry, so you can directly follow any concept that you find particularly interesting. This is as close to hypertext as I could get on a printed page.

Mentoring is sometimes stressful, but always joyful. Close contact with beginners keeps our own minds young. And through them, we touch the future. I hope this book serves you well!

— Judy Harrow

You who seek me,
know that all your seeking and yearning
will not avail
unless you know the mystery.
If you do not find what you seek within you
you will never find it elsewhere.
For, behold, I have been with you
since the beginning
and I shall be with you
until the end of days.

— adapted from the *Charge of the Goddess*

A Path of Our Own

CHAPTER 1

WHAT MAKES PAGANISM DIFFERENT

IT IS OFTEN SAID THAT ALL ROADS LEAD TO THE CENTER.
Perhaps they do. But the view from each road is different. Each
road has different landmarks and different pitfalls, and is best
suited to the capabilities or likings of different travelers. Pagan
mentors need to give some thought to what is different, even
special, about the Pagan cluster of spiritual paths.

First, it's important to know that there are indeed many good
paths. What is right for us is not necessarily right for everybody.

Historically, people have constructed a wide variety of myth
systems and theologies — the bases for many different religions
— then related to these human constructions as though they were
sets of objective facts about Deity, testable observations that can
be, at least theoretically, at least relatively, proven true or false.
When processes or things are observable and testable, reasonable
people can compare their observations, replicate each others'
experiments, and agree on the results. That's science.

But religion isn't science. We can't test and replicate our experiences of Deity because the Sacred is ultimately beyond human
comprehension and description. Both honesty and humility compel
us to admit that our knowledge of Deity is necessarily limited.

What glimpses we may get are also inevitably filtered through
lenses such as culture, class, gender, etc., each introducing its own
distortion. Denying these constraints and taking our specula-
tions as literal fact can cause great harm.

I live in metropolitan New York. I am writing in the autumn of
2001. My neighbors and I have recent and terrible experience of

actions impelled by fundamentalism. Fundamentalism is always presumption, always bigotry — and many times in human history has become the justification for mass murder.

Modern transportation and communication — most recently the Internet — have made it impossible to live in isolation. If we can truly accept that no one culture and no one mythos holds a monopoly on Sacred Truth, we can learn to live together in peace. Failing that, the culture wars will continue. My hope is that the same pluralism that makes tolerance necessary will also make peace possible by forcing us to notice that there are good people — and corrupt ones — in every faith community.

Pluralism induces other changes as well. What's importantly different for all of us in the English-speaking world at the beginning of the twenty-first century is that we now have access to so many more models of Deity, so many more systems of religious practice than any previous generation has had since the Roman Empire fell and indigenous European religions succumbed to the advance of an intolerant monotheism. Religious choice has been restored to us. With it, inevitably, comes responsibility for the choices that we make.

Contemporary Paganism is still mostly a first-generation religion. Most of us are here by conscious, adult choice. We have chosen a way that was long neglected. The forest trails are overgrown, even washed away in spots. We need to rebuild a few of the bridges and draw some new maps. It's hard work. If our path were not significantly different from the well-marked, well-trodden paths of our birth traditions, why would we not have continued in those easier ways?

So just what *is* different or special about neo-Pagan religious ideas?

We have no dogma, no required beliefs, no central authority figure. Nobody can impose uniformity of belief or practice upon us, and may all the Gods forbid that anyone ever could! I can only speak for myself. This is some of what I have personally worked out in a quarter century of study and practice and reflection:

1. WE ARE POLYTHEISTS.

The first thing people seem to notice about us, the most obvious difference, is that we are Goddess worshipers. Wiccans, in particular, offer our primary devotion to our beautiful, wounded, and threatened Mother Earth — and Wiccans are the best-known of the neo-Pagan groups. Indeed, She is central in my own life and work. But in a broader and deeper understanding of Paganism, Goddess worship is just an application of our radical polytheism.

I am a polytheist, not because I presume to define the Sacred as either plural or singular, but because of my understanding of the human religious imagination. Most polytheistic faith traditions actually postulate an unknown God, a "God behind the Gods," a Brahma, a Bondye, a Sacred Source that surpasses our human perceptual or conceptual abilities. This, which pervades and includes all, leaves nobody out and condones no discrimination or oppression.

But the human religious imagination seems to require personifications. Most of us, in order to relate to the Sacred, in order to pray at all, need to stick a face onto God. So we imagine, which means we create mental images. We build these models, these masks, because our minds cannot encompass the Whole of which we ourselves are but a part.

When people build such a model within the context of monotheism, it's likely to be a single model. Whatever models of Deity we adhere to are then also likely to become models for legitimate authority within our communities. Single models suggest that there's just one way to be holy, or at least that some kinds of people are closer to the holy than others. It's just another sad example of what happens when people take their myths literally. But it has practical repercussions.

For a long time in male monotheism, only men were admitted to the clergy or to religious leadership roles. This restriction commonly extended to secular leadership roles as well. The long struggle for women's ordination, which is nothing but simple justice, is not yet completely won. A few of the more retrogressive faith communities still discriminate against dedicated and gifted women who feel called to serve. At their annual meeting in 2000, the Southern Baptist Convention, a major American Protestant denomination, actually voted to cease ordaining women to their clergy, reversing a generation of nondiscriminatory practice. The Taliban had the same patriarchal bias, only stronger.

Watching such actions, we realize that none of us will ever be truly validated or securely empowered until we can find "a God that looks like me." While the One God in abstract can certainly be all-inclusive, once Deity "looks like" anybody in particular — stern white-bearded Father, loving giving Mother, or any other — most of us are left out. Patriarchal hierarchies are the logical outcome of male monotheist images of Deity.

We are not immune to similar blunders. Goddess monotheism can be just as disparaging to our men. Or an overemphasis on the generous Mother could be taken as an excuse to deny menopausal women the leadership roles appropriate to their rich experience.

In contrast, whole-hearted Paganism honors the diversity of Divinity and the divinity of diversity. Our many Gods — or, if you prefer, many models of the Sacred — show us an inclusive holiness that crosses all lines: gender, age, occupation — whatever. Our Deities — and our clergy — look like us.

Polytheism carries a risk of its own: loss of focus. Just as monotheistic abstraction turns out to be unsustainable in practice, so does unbounded polytheism. For daily practice, most of us are really henotheists. This arcane theological term describes people who, while acknowledging and honoring many gods, devote themselves to a very few, often just to one. While henotheistic practice may look a lot like monotheism, the difference between them is profound. The difference is choice. Henotheism and the choices it requires complicate the mentoring process in interesting ways. More on that later.

2. OUR SPIRITUALITY IS IMMANENCE-BASED BUT GOES BEYOND SIMPLE IMMANENCE.

Humans wonder. Humans speculate. Humans tell stories that metaphorically show what cannot be rationally explained, conveying a deeper-than-verbal intuition about how things are, about what is good or evil, about what is Sacred. We try our best to live by these stories, and perhaps make up more stories to explain our failures. Eventually, we reflect upon the entire collection of stories and our experiences of living by them, trying to abstract some more general principles from them. This we call *theology*, which literally means *God-talk*, discussion of the Sacred.

Theologies, systems of thought about Deity, have tended to cluster around two antithetical poles: transcendence and immanence. From the perspective of transcendence, the World of Spirit and the World of Form are entirely separate, perhaps even opposed to one another. Immanence, in radical contrast, finds the Sacred in the heart of the manifest world, here and now. If these were our only choices, contemporary Paganism would surely opt for the immanence perspective — we often refer to our faith as an Earth religion or Nature religion.

But when you follow the two ideas to their logical conclusions, they are just not really satisfying. Neither quite corresponds with our experience of spirituality, lived within this World of Form and open to Infinite Potential. Fortunately, a synthesis has emerged. It's called *panentheism*.

You may be familiar with a very similar word: *pantheism*. It means roughly the same thing as immanence: the identification of Deity with the existent universe. Panentheism is the belief that Spirit both pervades *and* transcends the World of Form; the two are like concentric circles. In short, panentheism holds that Deity includes the entire universe — and more. The World of Spirit is the world of all possibilities. The World of Form contains those possibilities which have become manifest. But these actualities, including humankind, could not exist without life-giving Spirit both at their innermost core and as their constitutive matrix.

Polytheism and panentheism are very abstract words representing very abstract theological principles. Are they just something to keep us head-trippers happily occupied while the true mystics trance and dream? I don't think so. These are the lenses through which we view Deity. They are what make us specifically Pagan and not just generically religious.

Pause for another vocabulary lesson. The Greek word *Entheos* refers to the indwelling Deity, the God of panentheism. Notice that the two words *Entheos* and *panentheism* share a similar root, which is also the root of the English word *enthusiasm*. But it's a singular word, so it cannot yet fully express a Pagan sense of the many-formed Sacred. The plural form is *Entheoi*, the indwelling Gods, the Ancient Ones who live and move in our hearts today as They did for our earliest ancestors.

Being Pagan, being devoted to the Entheoi, makes a big difference in our understandings of spiritual growth and of the ways to seek such growth or to assist others in their search. Power and pleasure, both suspect in other religious systems, are sacraments for us.

SPIRITUAL MENTORING

The word *sacrament* comes from the same Latin root as the words *sacred* and *consecrate*. Christians usually define it as a visible sign of invisible grace. In Church usage, the sacraments are a small number of very important rituals. But I think this more general definition works better for us: sacraments offer experiential evidence of Sacred Presence. At sacramental moments, both in and out of ritual, we can perceive the proximity of the Entheoi far more intensely than usual. At sacramental moments, for us, Spirit shines through Form.

For those in transcendence-based faith traditions, Spirit and Form are utterly separate. The manifest world is conceived of as illusory at best, possibly because we perceive it through imperfect human senses and even more imperfect human interpretive frameworks. Furthermore, the manifest world is constantly changing. All that lives eventually dies. Even the mountains go through their (much longer) cycles of eruption and erosion. You can't rely on any thing. Only God is eternal and unchanging.

Going further, some believe that Spirit and Form are not just radically different, but mutually opposed. For some, we are pure spirits ensnared in decaying matter, perhaps over many lifetimes, striving for liberation from the burden of a body. Others believe that pleasures of the flesh, even when not evil in themselves, distract us from a pure contemplative focus on the Sacred. To their understanding, we will not find the One unless we disconnect from the other.

These individuals turn to asceticism, believing it to be a vehicle for their path. Some practice simple self-deprivation: fasting, celibacy, or refusal to listen to music. Others actively "mortify the flesh." The literature of mysticism contains some lurid descriptions of what people have done to themselves in their quest for Sacred Contact. Note that I am not talking about the persecution of heretics, but of entirely voluntary, self-inflicted pain

-28-

and injury. I am also not talking about faraway times or exotic lands.

Desacralizing the manifest world has also led directly to our present environmental crisis. Just as human bodies are regarded as objects to be subdued, so the Earth Herself is conceived of as just a thing without intrinsic holiness or value, to be conserved — if at all — only because enlightened self-interest demands wise use.

Panentheism impels us to an entirely different approach. For us, the Entheoi dwell within this life, in these bodies, on this Earth, here and now. The beauties of nature and of human art are sacraments for us, windows through which Spirit shines. One of the core texts of Wicca, the Charge of the Goddess, teaches us that "all acts of love and pleasure are Her rituals." If they are, then asceticism is nothing less than the sin of ingratitude.

So, as a Pagan mentor, I am much more likely to suggest that a student eat an orange or listen to music with reverent attention than that they sleep on a hard board without blankets.

The Charge of the Goddess also teaches us that beauty is complemented and balanced by strength. Appropriately then, personal power is another of our Pagan sacraments.

For some faith traditions, human will is the very substance of sin, and holiness consists of total personal submission to the will of the Deity. To practice and develop this submissive attitude, monastics take vows of obedience. The same ascetic practices that promote dissociation from the senses are also intended to extinguish any personal tastes or preferences, so that the personality can be entirely subsumed in God.[1]

Gerald May is a psychiatrist, and was formerly supervisor of a highly respected training program for Christian spiritual directors. His book *Will and Spirit* lauds "willingness," by which he means utter self-surrender, and disparages "willfulness," his term for self-assertion and goal-seeking behavior. For May, all spiritual experience is pure grace, an undeserved gift. Even our ability to submit to God's will is a manifestation of God's grace, granted only to some. Human effort towards spiritual growth is irrelevant and probably counterproductive. Here's a typical example:

> Any attempt to accomplish something spiritual is self-defeating. All one can do is encourage one's willingness for something to happen. . . . In our willful, manipulation-addicted society it is not surprising that one would try to make unitive experiences happen. It is even less surprising in view of the fact that such experiences so often seem to be "triggered" by certain environmental or psychological situations. This observation makes it almost impossible for us *not* to jump to the conclusion that some cause-and-effect relationship does exist and that we could master and control it if we only knew how. To date, however, such attempts have at best succeeded in achieving only pieces of unitive experience. The full thing has not been, and the contemplatives would say *cannot* be achieved.[2]

From May's theological perspective, within his understanding of the relationship between Deity and humankind, this makes complete sense. In profound contrast, let me suggest a possible Pagan interpretation. Obviously, some people have reliable conscious contact with Deity and others do not. If such contact is pure grace, if human effort matters not a whit, then it follows that Deity plays favorites. Indeed, the Bible that May's faith community relies on contains, in the Book of Job, an appalling portrayal of a capricious and unfair Deity whose only response to a battered worshiper's questions about justice is a display of raw power.

If, on the other hand, the Entheoi pervade and nurture all life, then we all have the same access to Sacred Contact. The only difference is whether we make ourselves conscious of this contact and whether we live our lives in congruence with the power and guidance that we derive from it. That difference places the initiative — and the responsibility — squarely with each seeker. By focus and will, by both seeking the inner light and acting in accordance, we make the Entheoi manifest in all parts of ourselves and our lives. We ourselves become the sacrament.

Which view is factual? Does spiritual growth start with and depend upon Call or Quest? Once again, simplistic answers just dissolve upon close examination.

To the extent that a mystic's quest stems from some personality trait, some special aptitude or drive for Sacred Contact, we might say that genetic endowment is given or graced. If personality is understood to be molded by family and culture, if religious motivations come from our upbringing, then we might say that people are placed in families and communities by Sacred Wisdom, so again we come to grace. Trace any causal sequence back far enough and you will glimpse the Entheoi, particularly if your guiding model is that of panentheism.

This controversy about whether spiritual exploration originates with quest or call, effort or grace, is simply a theological application of the old social science debate between autonomy and determinism. Once again the real question is not which model is factual, but rather which model is most useful. The issue can never be definitively resolved because both insights are correct. The proportion may vary from one person to the next or according to what we are trying to understand or accomplish at the moment. And is light a particle or a wave?

For a mentor or a seeker, it's most useful to consider spiritual growth as a quest. Divine love is constant and given, and the proof of this is that we live at all. We cannot control it and do not need to, for it is not arbitrary or capricious. Our own behavior is what we can change, and changing that can require a good deal of hard and sometimes uncomfortable inner work. Thinking of the process as a quest, a path, encourages us to make the effort, to return to the path when we have been sidetracked (perhaps bringing to it what we learned along the detour), to rest when we need to, to get up when we stumble, to keep on keeping on.

As Pagans, we take responsibility for our own decisions and actions, for our own growth. Pride is a sin — in somebody else's religion.

By will and by acting in accordance with that will, we also make changes in the manifest world. Magic is the art of causing change in accordance with will. Another of the most obvious things about us, and one that has long made us the objects of fear, suspicion, and even hatred, is that we are magic users.

Just as with pleasure, many faith traditions teach that magic and spirituality are completely different, maybe even directly opposite. The milder opinion is that, while pursuing spiritual development will open up some psychic powers, these are just a distraction from the main event, a side road to be bypassed along the path. They aren't bad in themselves, but they compete for the seeker's limited time and energy.

For those who define spirituality as the total submission of the personal will to the Divine will, magic is not just a distraction. They perceive it as being antithetical to spiritual growth — a bad thing. Magic users train, clarify, and focus will. We project our will into the world to bring change. We are actively and intentionally willful, and we make no apology for this.

For us, the experience of working magic is the experience of participating in the living power of the Entheoi. To perform a healing is an even greater sacrament than to receive one.

Power and pleasure can be taken to both unhealthy and unbalanced extremes. Overeating to the point where the body's health is endangered is an obvious example. So is using personal power to coerce or exploit others. Indeed, this is what our neighbors fear. However, Wiccans share a core ethic, a "golden rule" of our path, which also deeply influences the wider Pagan community. We call it the Wiccan Rede. It states:

Eight words the Wiccan Rede fulfill:
An it harm none, do what you will.

We'll be exploring the implications of the Rede throughout the book. For now, please notice how the Rede clearly affirms human will, bounded only by consideration and respect. A Pagan path has no place for any needless restriction of power, pleasure, or pride. Ours is the path of freedom, the way of joy.

TO LEARN MORE

These sources are good introductions to theological reflection for Pagans:

Bednarowski, Mary Farrell. *New Religions and the Theological Imagination in America*. Bloomington: Indiana University Press, 1989. ISBN 025321338X

In describing how six new religions answer some of the more common religious questions, Bednarowski gives us some starting points for developing our own answers.

Christ, Carol P. *Rebirth of the Goddess: Finding Meaning in Feminist Spirituality*. New York: Routledge, 1997. ISBN 0415921864

This book looks at Goddess worship through the lens of Christian-influenced systematic theology. Christ does a pretty good job of fitting our faith into that framework. It's a starting point, a model for theological reflection. As we mature, I think we'll need to develop our own analytical categories.

diZerega, Gus. *Pagans & Christians: The Personal Spiritual Experience.* St. Paul: Llewellyn, 2001. ISBN 1567182283

Kudos to Gus diZerega for the first modern book of Pagan theology. He also does a lot to promote better Pagan/Christian understanding. It is both erudite and accessible, and I recommend that you make this book your first priority.

Eck, Diana L. *A New Religious America.* San Francisco: HarperSanFrancisco, 2001. ISBN 0060621591

Eck is the director of the Diversity Project at the Harvard Divinity School. Her book traces the evolution of America from an essentially Christian culture to one that is religiously diverse. It includes fascinating descriptions of the interplay between early immigration, conversion, recent immigration, and the ways in which the children of recent immigrants are balancing their dual identities.

These sources are a basic introduction to liberal theology, presented in the sequence that I recommend you read them in, so that the ideas can build on each other:

Geertz, Clifford. "Religion as a Cultural System." In *The Interpretation of Cultures*, 87–125. New York: Basic Books, 1973. ISBN 0465097197

Geertz gives a clear and practical starting point for understanding what religion is and how it functions in human life. His definition: "a religion is a system of symbols which acts to establish powerful, pervasive and long-lasting moods and motivations by formulating conceptions of a general order of existence and clothing these conceptions with such an aura of factuality that the moods and motivations seem uniquely realistic." The essay explains each term in the definition in careful detail.

Christ, Carol P. "Why Women Need the Goddess." In *Womanspirit Rising: A Feminist Reader in Religion*, edited by Carol P. Christ and Judith Plaskow, 273–87. San Francisco: Harper & Row, 1979. ISBN 0060613777

Applies Geertz's theory to the religious needs of modern, feminist women. This essay has been reprinted several times. It's worth trying to find a copy of the original anthology, however, because it really set the tone for the emerging field of feminist theology.

Ruether, Rosemary R. *Sexism and God-Talk*. Boston: Beacon, 1983. ISBN 080701205X

Because this is a Christian book, it may not seem particularly relevant. It is, however, if you read it to observe Ruether's method. For each major theological question, she first assesses the resources within the Christian tradition. Some of these she finds useful, others hopelessly contaminated by sexism. Then she looks further for useable material, some of which she finds in the Goddess Traditions. Ruether's approach shows us how to treat inherited texts as precious resources but not as infallible and invariant intellectual fetters.

Downing, Christine. *The Goddess: Mythological Images of the Feminine*. New York: Crossroad, 1984. ISBN 0826409172

Downing concentrates on the Greek Goddesses. There's a long, juicy chapter on each one. Even if you're not focused on the Greeks, this book is valuable for the model it provides for working with any specific Deity. In each case, Downing draws on the source material about the Deity and then connects it with her own life issues.

Brown, Karen McCarthy. *Mama Lola: A Vodou Priestess in Brooklyn*. Berkeley: University of California Press, 1991. ISBN 0520224752

Brown uses a similar approach to Downing's, applying it to the loa spirits of Haitian Vodou. She alternates chapters: one looks at a particular loa in great depth and the next examines how that loa's energy shows up in the experience of the family Brown studied, and in Haitian society in general. This work is particularly important for Pagans because Vodou, although now syncretized with Christianity, has clear continuous roots in African indigenous religion.

Friedrich, Paul. *The Meaning of Aphrodite*. Chicago: University of Chicago Press, 1978. ISBN 0226264831

Friedrich's volume demonstrates how concepts of Aphrodite evolved and changed over the centuries in consonance with changes in human culture.

NOTES

[1] James William, *The Varieties of Religious Experience* (1902; reprint, New York: Collier, 1961), 249–52.
[2] Gerald F. May, *Will and Spirit* (New York: HarperCollins, 1982), 58.

Traveling Companions

CHAPTER 2

MENTOR AND STUDENT

FOR MY FIRST THREE MONTHS OF COLLEGE, THE ENTIRE freshman class met each week with the Dean of Students for a series of workshops on adjustment to college life. These covered general topics such as study techniques and time management. Then, from Thanksgiving till the end of the semester, we broke into small discussion groups to address more personal concerns. Each group met with a different faculty member — mine with the college chaplain. He was my first spiritual mentor. He remains one of my chosen spiritual ancestors, my personal "Mighty Dead."

The group I was in met weekly in the chapel office for intense discussions, sometimes about issues in our lives and more often about the books our adviser recommended. These books and discussions introduced me to the whole exciting field of contemporary theology and situational ethics. They helped me understand that the various religions really do have very different perspectives on the nature of humanity and Deity and their proper relationship. It was in these weekly meetings that I learned to think critically about religious issues. Although the chaplain and I were not of the same religion, he helped me truly appreciate the one I was born into — and prepared me for that joyous but wrenching moment when I would discover that neo-Paganism met my needs far better.

Freshman orientation concluded at the end of the first semester, but my discussion group continued to meet weekly, on a completely voluntary basis, during our entire first two years. The chaplain got no extra pay. We got no extra credits. What we got from that group experience was far more valuable: intellectual stimulation and spiritual nurturance.

In November of my sophomore year, President Kennedy was assassinated. All campus activities stopped abruptly. Most people had no idea what to do next. My discussion group, then about a year old, instinctively gathered in the chapel office, which had become our home base on campus. We spent the afternoon planning a special interfaith chapel service for that evening, hoping it would help people cope with their loss and grief. By working to comfort others, we calmed and comforted ourselves. The chaplain's quiet presence was the centerpoint from which this healing emanated. Almost forty years later and a Priestess myself, I reached back to his example for guidance when the Twin Towers fell in New York.

Mentoring is both a relationship and an activity. The relationship is more important because the goal of the activity is personal development rather than either training or education. Information can be shared without any personal relationship; all of us have learned from books or from broadcast documentaries. Skills can be transferred from one person to another through very narrow interactions; I can learn how to bake bread or write a computer program quite well from a person who is otherwise dysfunctional. But only a truly spiritual person can show another how to become spiritual — and not by precept, only by example.

That discussion group was never intended to teach us how to mentor. If anything, the chaplain's intention was to teach us something about theology, ethics, and values. And even that was incidental to offering us a place to share our feelings about adjusting to college life. But, by his presence and his ways of interacting with us, the chaplain *showed* us how to mentor. Before any mentor can guide students along any inner growth path, student and mentor must establish a relationship of respect and trust. Over time, as they work well together, trust will ripen into love. Love and trust will nurture growth — for both mentor and student.

THE MENTOR

What does the elder bring to the mentoring relationship? What innate talents and temperaments? What knowledge and which skills? Who should take on this important role?

Before reading further, please take a moment to think about those elders you remember with gratitude and love. Maybe it was a schoolteacher who, while teaching their subject, also taught you how to think clearly, how to learn. Maybe it was a parent or grandparent who shared kindness and commonsense wisdom along with domestic skills. Maybe it was a clergy member in your birth tradition who demonstrated guiding values and Sacred Presence. Maybe it was the friend who showed you the inconspicuous entry to the Pagan path. Very likely it was several different people at different points in your life. Whoever it was, remember now how it was between you and them, how they touched and changed your life. What did they bring to the process?

Spirituality is not a skill, although there are skills that support it. Spirituality is the quest for conscious connection with Deity. Nobody can teach what they do not know. Nobody can share what they do not have. A spiritual mentor is, and must be, primarily a role model, a person who is actively pursuing their own advanced spiritual development. Everything else arises from this sturdy base.

A person who mentors within a specific faith tradition should ideally be an elder practitioner of that tradition with a broad and deep knowledge of its lore. But our religion is *neo*-Paganism: ancient indeed but new to us, newly emerged from centuries of dormancy.

Today our faith group is one of the fastest growing in North America. Even though we do not proselytize, we have more new seekers than we have elders who can teach them. As a result, many Pagan mentors are not much more than advanced beginners. I, for example, had just four years of experience when I began to teach, and that's not at all unusual. My own beloved High Priestess was just about four years ahead of me.

I'm painfully aware that my present students are getting much more than that first brave group ever did. I have learned so much in twenty years, both about our path and about teaching. It would be a shame if I had not. Still, it's better for a seeker to have a good-hearted but relatively inexperienced human mentor, who can answer questions or point out interesting sights, than to wander the path all alone. A traveling companion is much more helpful than the best map. The good college chaplain graduated from seminary the same year I graduated from high school. He was new to the ministry when our discussion group began, just starting his first job. Yet he effectively nurtured our development.

If you feel called to mentor others but lack experience, don't let false modesty inhibit you from doing this much-needed work. Please remember that many of the best workers in any field suffer from *impostor syndrome*, the fear of their own incompetence. In fact, this fear drives them to keep learning, to keep growing, and that's precisely how they become the best.

Don't exaggerate your background. That's not fair to potential students or to the community. You can draw confidence from the reality that even what the utter beginner can offer is much better than nothing. Try to find some good elder and/or peer support. If there's nobody nearby, you can still connect pretty well through the Internet.[1] Think of yourself as a graduate teaching assistant. Let yourself learn the lessons of experience, even though some are hard. That's how we can do the best job for the most people.

On the other hand, there is no need for you to be a mentor at all unless you feel the inner call to this work. Never allow yourself to be seduced or pressured into taking on this demanding role. There are many, many other worthy ways for an elder to contribute to the Pagan renaissance, many ways to feel good about yourself and to earn the respect of your peers.

During the centuries of Pagan dormancy, a lot of our traditional lore was lost. For this reason, it particularly behooves Pagan mentors to learn about much more than Paganism. Studying the spirituality and mysticism of other faith communities helps us understand our own. We ought to pay special attention to those indigenous cultures that kept their religious lifeways intact centuries longer than our own, some even continuously to this day. What we learn from them can help fill the gaps. There are scholarly works on the study of myth and ritual, the psychology of religion, the history of religion, and much more. Most recently, serious Pagan scholarship has started to become available. We need to gather for ourselves the best possible knowledge base, and that means hunting far beyond the standard "occult" or "new age" sources.

Information of this sort can help us reflect on our primary religious experience, and such reflection is essential. Visionary experience without understanding, critical thinking, and discernment puts us at risk for fanaticism and delusion.

However, purely academic knowledge can never replace primary religious experience. Consider this: I could study and teach any religion abstractly, from a purely intellectual basis. I could read a lot of sources, maybe even interview some people or observe some rituals. I could develop some understanding and then communicate it to others in writing or in a lecture. I could do all this, diligently and competently, without ever engaging with the material I study on any deep level or using it for my own spiritual development. I could properly research and clearly explain even some acts I find repugnant and would personally never do. But I can't serve another as companion and guide along a path I have not walked myself.

We need to engage both head and heart to travel our path well. There's a huge difference between "knowing" and "knowing about" something. Reading the most excellent travel book is not the same as going somewhere in person. Information is not an end in itself, nor even a direct means to that end — just a resource. A professor of Pagan religious studies is not necessarily a mentor.

People skills are also utterly vital to the mentoring relationship. A good mentor's guiding ethic is service to the student, the community, and the Gods. A competent mentor is able to assess people, to identify those who have the proper motivations and talents for spiritual exploration, and to monitor their progress on the path. With this comes an understanding of some of the typical issues that arise in the course of human psycho-spiritual growth. A wise mentor will have some sense of when to intervene and when to stand aside and allow the student to learn even from the difficult experience of making mistakes. They should also be conversant with available resources, and able to suggest books to read or exercises to try that will help the student grow.

Communication is what makes and maintains relationship. A good mentor must be willing and able to listen to the student actively and empathetically, to speak to the student gently, clearly, and honestly — but also to say what is necessary, even when this is uncomfortable for both speaker and listener.

Most challenging and difficult of all, the mentor becomes, for a while, a sort of ideal role model for the student. To understand this occurrence, we need to borrow a concept from secular psychotherapy: the *idealizing transference*.[2]

Transference is the psychological process by which emotions and desires originally associated with someone in our past — usually a family member — are unconsciously shifted to (or projected on to) someone in our present. For example, people may act out with their therapists (or clergy) issues that originated with their parents or other caregivers. They may act out with members of their congregation or group issues that originated with siblings or childhood friends. Therapists are trained to bear these transferences (or manage those that come up in groups) to allow clients to resolve the old issues and move on in their lives. Clergy, even those who are seminary trained, are not usually so prepared.

Idealizing transference is a related, but different, process. Instead of projecting old troubles in order to work through them, people project new hopes in order to work towards them. By imagining that another person — perhaps a therapist or priest/ess — embodies their desires and aspirations, people convince themselves that these goals are really achievable. That belief empowers their efforts.

Idealizing transference is even more likely to happen in spiritual mentoring than it is in secular therapy. The mentor is not just seen as living well, but as living in closer conscious contact with Deity, as actually being holier. If our mentors are holy, then holiness is a goal that we, too, can hope to achieve. The mentor's demonstrated belief in the student's potential for spiritual growth is another important piece of evidence.

The student's idealizing transference catches the mentor in a web of paradox.

- Mentors have to earn and deserve their students' trust. We have to actually *be* caring and competent, like any secular counselor who carries their clients' idealizing transference. More than that, spiritual mentors have to be authentic role models for advanced, wholesome, and continuing spiritual growth, and for lives lived in accordance with deeply held values. We have to embody and demonstrate the joyous possibilities of a spirit-filled life.

- Mentors have to tolerate carrying our students' ideals. Students will put us up on pedestals. Pedestals are uncomfortable places, lonely and frightening. We see ourselves from the inside, and live with ourselves full time. Students who see us in mentoring sessions or ritual settings, for which we have carefully prepared, may not know that we're also grumpy in the morning or impatient with slow supermarket cashiers. So we feel inauthentic, even hypocritical, allowing students to hold on to these flattering false images. We dread the moment they discover the truth — and impostor syndrome can amplify that fear. Nevertheless, we must set our discomfort aside and bear the projections long enough for the student to gain some confidence and momentum in their own development.

- Mentors must never come to need our students to idealize us. As frightening as the pedestal is at first, it's also frighteningly easy to get used to being up there. Whoever carries the idealizing projections of others can begin to believe in them and to enjoy the deference they elicit. If we succumb to this temptation, we put our own spiritual health in danger along with that of our students. Needy mentors will probably develop patterns of people-pleasing and codependency. They will find it difficult to confront students on inconsistent or inappropriate behavior. They will be weak, and come across as weak, depriving students of exactly the perception of safety and security that they so need. At the same time, the needy mentor comes to believe the students' projections, thus risking ego inflation, a false sense of entitlement, and actual corruption. We've seen too many gurus fall that way.

The idealizing transference is one of those dangerous good things, like fire. We have to deserve it and endure it, without ever coming to want it. We have to carry those impossible projections for a while, then gently but firmly hand them back to the student. Mature spirituality is not dependent on wise elders or even on sacred texts and traditions, but on conscious contact with the Entheoi. Students start by depending on their mentors, but grow into autonomy and self-reliance. They find what they truly seek — contact with the Entheoi — within themselves or nowhere.

The role of mentor is demanding but also rewarding. By our loving support, our trusting challenge, and our reliable commitment, we make real differences in the spiritual lives of our students and, student by student, help keep the Pagan renaissance growing.

THE STUDENT

We'll explore the mentoring process in more detail in Chapter 3. For now, let's turn to the student, the other half of the relationship.

Our Pagan community is growing so fast right now. No mentor can effectively serve all the potential students, so choices must be made. Who are these seekers, anyhow? How do you choose among them? Which seeker will benefit most from your kind of spirituality and in time become a contributing member of the faith community? Which student's learning style meshes best with your personal way of teaching? Which student's core values best match your own?

The mentoring relationship works best when mentor and student are most compatible. Before you can know which students you can mentor best, you need to know something about yourself, your values, your perspectives on our religion, and your ways of working with people. If you are a relatively new mentor, your learning style can give you some insight into what your teaching style is likely to become.

You may have done extensive self-assessment during your own period of training. If not, now's the time. Even if you did, you probably should check for changes. Here are some of the kinds of things you may want to know about yourself to help you choose compatible students:

- What is your personal learning and/or teaching style?
- What are your core spiritual or magical values?
- What is your central expertise? Which skills or specialties do you feel best qualified to teach to others?
- In your opinion, how is your Tradition or path currently developing or improving? Are there other ways you believe your Tradition or path might or should improve?
- Which current trends in your Tradition or path do you dislike? How would you seek to counter them?
- What kinds of attitudes and behaviors do you find particularly admirable or offensive in a co-religionist?

Because of our rapid growth, we are largely a first-generation religion, a community of converts. This creates an additional complication for Pagan mentors, since *conversion* means at least two different things. It might mean a simple change of religious affiliation, a sort of lateral transfer. It might also mean a promotion to more intense participation in the same religion, when a person "converts" from conventional, exoteric, "lay" practice to a far more intense esoteric or mystical approach. It could even be both at once.

Understanding these two different meanings of the word *conversion* may help clarify our perennial and painful debates about working with seekers who are teenagers, legal minors.

Some of us advocate turning young people away from even open, public Sabbat celebrations unless they have parental consent. One concern is that offended parents will bring charges against us or sue us or something. In some jurisdictions, that might still actually happen. Even if we lost the trial, we'd surely win the appeal. Have you ever seen unaccompanied young folks being carded at the entry to a church or synagogue? The real problem, of course, is that winning such a case can leave a person bankrupt.

Another concern is publicity, especially in smaller towns. Irate parents might cause the kind of public scandal that would lead to ostracism, harassment — even of our own small children — loss of jobs or business, and other unpleasant extralegal consequences. Our best magic won't mend broken windows. Turning non-Pagan teens away may be pragmatic and may avoid a lot of trouble, but it can't be right.

Adolescent children are neither the property nor the puppets of their parents. Religious exploration is a normal part of adolescent identity formation. Mainstream religions traditionally place the age of religious responsibility a few years prior to the current age of legal majority. Jewish youngsters make their Bat or Bar Mitzvah at thirteen. Catholics, too, are confirmed in their early teens. Some adventurous youngsters may find their way to us.

We don't proselytize — not with people of any age. We are willing to live and let live, and ask that others extend the same respect to us. But most of us remember what it was like to discover that we were not alone after all, that there was a faith tradition and a community that fit our own needs and values. Among ourselves, we don't call this *conversion* at all; we call it *homecoming*. When a teenager finds their way home to the Old Ways, can we in all conscience send them away? What happens if we do? If it meant nothing worse than a delay, we could frame it as a frustrating test of motivation and sincerity. But it's a dangerous delay.

If we reject them, they will still explore on their own. Without responsible guidance, they may run into trouble. Their experimentation may bring on overwhelming inner experiences, "spiritual emergencies," without easy access to experienced elders who can help them understand and integrate the experience. Worse yet, they may come into contact with charlatans or predators, unscrupulous people who use the trappings of religion to exploit or hurt the vulnerable young. All religions attract such scum at their margins.

If we welcome teenage seekers, they will be in a position similar to that of those very few youngsters who were raised in Pagan families. Birthright Pagan or homecomer, the second type of conversion to intense inner exploration can and should usually wait until the storms of adolescence have subsided and the young adult is ready, willing, and able to make a mature commitment to that path.

The person who intensifies their practice of the same religion will already know the basic stories, symbols, and rituals of that path. They are well grounded in the ethics that spring from that religion's core values. They have built a good container for the inspiration they hope to receive. In fact, some religions — Judaism and Hinduism, for example — advise adherents to defer mystical exploration until their mature years, when the demanding tasks of launching a career, building a marriage, and raising young children are also settling down.

Pagan adults who are deepening their commitment, should they seek your mentoring, will not need you to repeat their basic religious education. New Pagans of any age will need to start from the very beginning. So consider whether you have the patience to review the basics before you agree to mentor new Pagans. In the secular world, different temperaments and skills are required for those who teach grade school and those who teach grad school.

A generation ago, when there were fewer practicing Pagans and those few kept themselves much more hidden, only the strongly motivated found us. They tended to seek intense practice right away. My own Wiccan initiation took place less than a year after the first Sabbat ritual I ever attended. I made both moves at about the same time.

As neo-Paganism matures, public rituals become easier to find in more local areas. An increasing number of new Pagans ease in more gradually. They attend open rituals, but go no deeper for at least a while. Contrary to our own self-image, even our own ideology, we now have a laity.

The advent of this laity means that our community is maturing — not being diluted. The inner orders, such as the various Wiccan Traditions, still offer intense practice to the motivated. Their percentage of the general Pagan population is getting smaller because their growth is relatively slower, as it should be. They are still definitely growing. The presence of a vibrant laity gives the inner orders more potential candidates to choose from, as it gives newcomers time to get acclimated to a new religious context before undertaking deep explorations.

Whoever eventually chooses to go deeper will probably already be familiar with the basics. This circumstance has raised expectations for both the mentor and the student. We are no longer teaching beginners; we are teaching advanced spiritual, priestly, and magical skills to people who seek a stronger, deeper religious experience of the Pagan path.

In assessing your own potential students, don't think of them as new members of our religion. Think of them as Pagans with new religious vocations, applying for apprenticeship with you as members of other faith communities might apply for admission to a seminary, convent, or monastery.

FINDING YOUR LIMITS

When a person requests mentoring, there are four possible responses. We can accept them. We can refer them to some other mentor. We can defer them, tell them "not yet," perhaps give them some suggestions about what they can work on in the interim. Or we can just plain reject them. Also, sometimes we know nearly immediately what we want to do; at other times we mull over our reactions for quite a while.

To get a sense of where your own preferences and limits lie, try to identify the extremes, the people whom you would accept or reject with only minimal consideration. Some typical examples follow. I don't personally agree with all of them, and you may not either. The important thing for now is to become conscious of your own limits.

You might immediately accept someone if:
- The seeker was recommended by someone you respect, perhaps your own elder.
- The seeker is an old and dear friend.
- The seeker was previously deferred. The reason you deferred them no longer applies. You feel obligated.

You might summarily reject someone if:

- The seeker is, in your opinion, immature or emotionally unstable.
- The seeker seems to want something you cannot or will not offer.
- The seeker seems too overloaded with other responsibilities and interests to devote the necessary time and energy to this work.
- The seeker is hostile towards your elders or your lifemate.
- The seeker is a legal minor without parental consent. You are concerned about the risk.
- The seeker is in a committed relationship. Their mate does not approve of their religious path.

In between the definite *yes* and the definite *no* comes the wide range of *maybe*. You'll meet seekers who seem quite acceptable, who certainly don't set off any inner alarms. But neither do you feel any great passion for working with them. You might pass those by. Many mentors would.

Or you might choose to work with some of them for a while and see what develops. If you do want to experiment with some of these "maybes," be mindful of your own limits of time, energy, and attention. You can't work this closely with more than a few people at a time. So you'll need to find a way to pick and choose from among the middle group. Here are some things to think about as you do.

First, beware of extrinsic reasons, those that are not directly relevant. Base your decision on the person's capacity and compatibility, not on incidentals. Be particularly cautious about allowing ulterior reasons tempt you into accepting a student who is really not well qualified or well matched. Beware of accepting a dubious seeker for reasons like these:

- The seeker has lots of money and is generous.
- You are physically or romantically attracted to the seeker.
- You feel that some other teacher mistreated this seeker. You would like to do better by them (and/or get one-up on someone you dislike).
- Some Big Name Pagan recommended the seeker to you. This gratifies your ego and impresses other local elders.
- You think that having a larger number of students will increase your status in the community.

So what are some more appropriate considerations? Clichés can encode a great deal of wisdom. In fact, that's how they *become* clichés. In deciding whether a person should start something new and major in their life, like spiritual exploration, it's useful to consider whether that person is — to draw on an old cliché — "ready, willing, and able." What do these three words mean for Pagan mentors?

1. Ready

Advanced Pagan spiritual development is not for everyone. It begins with deep self-confrontation, as we work through our own old "stuff" to open up a clear channel for the wisdom of the Gods. Not everyone is strong enough to face their own demons, the true "guardians at the gateway." Magical development gives a sorcerer powerful tools for intervening in the World of Form, tools which should be made available only to those who will use them with compassion, wisdom, respect, and restraint. High-energy workings can destabilize a fragile personality. Navigating altered states of consciousness endangers people who are not sufficiently anchored in ordinary reality to return and function there most of the time.

One of our working definitions of spirituality is creating,

sustaining, deepening, and clarifying our conscious contact with the Ancient Gods. A frequently used metaphor for this is opening a channel that connects us with the Entheoi. The existence of a channel implies some sort of flow. A useful term for the power, guidance, and blessing that flow through that channel is *awen*.

Awen is a Welsh word, usually translated as *poetic inspiration*. In the indigenous culture of Britain, however, bards were not understood as literary entertainers or even artists as most poets are today. Their role was closer to that of prophets or shamans. They spoke for the Gods, often from trance states. They brought the Sacred awen to the people.

The power of awen can overwhelm the unprepared recipient, throwing them into spiritual emergency. People in spiritual emergency often have trouble handling the normal activities and responsibilities of life. Although they are situationally and temporarily overwhelmed, they can be difficult to distinguish from those who are mentally ill. But a mentor is not a qualified psychotherapist.

Ethical practice requires you to acknowledge and honor the limits of your training and experience. Some people do have serious emotional impairments arising from terrible personal history or even from organic and physical malfunctions of the brain. Their need for healing services is very real, sometimes tragically real. You'll want to help, but this is one case where "fake it till you make it" just doesn't apply. The very best thing you can do for such a person is to help them find a Pagan-friendly clinician. In cases of serious mental illness, clinical competence is more important than religious tolerance.

Occasionally a seeker to whom you feel drawn will tell you that they have been diagnosed with a mental illness, but are controlling the symptoms through medication and therapy. They feel able to, and called to, go further along the path. What then?

First, I'd give that person a lot of credit for honesty and courage. By leveling with you, they are risking a painful rejection. Then I'd see if it's possible to talk with their therapist. If you can, establish a relationship so that you can let the therapist know, and seek their advice, if this student seems to be running into problems.

Whether or not direct consultation is an option, you most certainly should inform yourself about this person's condition. The National Institute for Mental Health makes some high-quality information available for free on the Internet at <www.nimh.nih.gov/publicat/index.cfm>. This is a service for the families of people with mental illness, so it contains information about how to support the therapeutic process and what symptoms are danger signals. These are exactly the sorts of things you need to know.

If, after learning all I could about their condition, I decided to proceed with a mentally ill person, I'd slow the process down as much as possible, allowing plenty of time for them to find their balance after each small step.

A person needs to be a sane, stable adult with a good sense of their own identity, boundaries, and ethics before they explore the esoteric aspects of this or any other religion, before they can safely seek or receive the awen. People who are already psychologically or emotionally fragile can be seriously and permanently damaged. Specifically, beware of:

- Seekers who seem unreliable. Seekers who are unable or unwilling to take responsibility for their mistakes. Seekers who think that every mistake is a catastrophe.
- Seekers who have trouble living in ordinary reality, in the "World of Form."
- Seekers who have a fragmented self or poor sense of personal identity and boundaries, who can't tell their own fantasies

from reality. They will have trouble integrating mystical experiences and may get lost in their own dreamworld. If they tell you, for example, that the reason they can't hold a job is because they are a member of an extraterrestrial priestly caste, beware.

• Seekers with poor impulse or anger control, especially if active magic is part of your path. Seekers whose primary motivation seems to be the acquisition of magical control over others.

• Seekers who tend to locate their problems outside themselves, especially those who blame their problems on curses, demons, or occult phenomena of any kind, and who are looking for some magical or occult fix for their problems.

• Seekers who don't (or don't yet) seem to be strong enough to deal with painful personal material that inner exploration will probably bring up.

Here's a more positive way of looking at readiness: Before entering a committed order of any religion, a person should be a mature and stable practitioner of that religion. What might religious maturity be for a Pagan? Chapter 4 will explore a variety of theories and models of personal spiritual development in some detail. For now, here's my personal shortlist. As you read it, think about how your own might be the same or different. I would be inclined to mentor people who:

• Love and care for Mother Earth.

• Know that Sacred Wisdom is to be found within, and accept the challenge of opening, deepening, and clarifying that inner channel.

• Actively seek personal development through meditation, ritual, and the nurturance of their own creative talents.

- Try to live in growing accordance with their best under-standing of what awen and Tradition teach, and who "walk their talk."
- Recognize that others may express Sacred Wisdom in different metaphors; honor diversity.
- Are open-minded and curious; recognize that there is always more room for learning and growth; are willing to respectfully test and challenge received wisdom.

2. Willing

Pagans honor individual will, regarding it as an essential compo-nent of our magic and our growth. Understanding something about a seeker's will — both its strength and its nature or direction — is a correspondingly important part of evaluating that seeker's potential as a student.

- Quantity: Are they motivated enough to really do all the work involved? This will be easy to tell as time goes on.
- Quality: Are their motivations appropriate? Do they want to go to the places you feel willing to guide them? This is a more subtle assessment, and far more important. Insufficient motivation may halt or delay development, wasting your time and theirs, but it will not move them in the wrong direction.

My best advice: simply ask the seeker, "How do you think I can help you? What are you hoping to find here?" If you get a super-ficial answer, ask again: "And how will that help you?" Ask until you've reached some depth. See how you feel about the response.

And ask yourself what *you* consider to be the right reasons to seek training. If your answer clashes with theirs, you probably won't do well together. For me, there are two right answers:

compassionate service or creative celebration. Or better yet, both. Genuine Sacred Contact always seems to flow into kindness and/or beauty.

From time to time, however, people will be drawn to our path by very understandable, but lesser, needs and desires. They may, for example, have some psychic talent that was ridiculed and ignored in the secular world, and are hoping for acceptance and perhaps a little help in understanding and managing their weird experiences. It can be very tempting to accept needy seekers out of charity, particularly if you have a need to be needed (a tendency towards codependency often drives "helpers").

Others are attracted to the Pagan community, and particularly to Wicca, because of our reputation as magic workers. They have not the slightest interest in Pagan spirituality. Instead, they hope to learn how to control other people for their own selfish advantage, accepting no ethical limits on the exercise of their personal will.

Will and power are both associated with fire. Like fire, they are dangerous goods. Unless they are bounded and balanced by respect for others and the desire to serve, they are corrupting to the person and corrosive to the community. Magic can be abused for coercive or manipulative purposes, but not with my help.

Some people come because they find a community that advocates and practices values they already hold. This is the classic "homecoming" experience, so often and so movingly described. Some come because they love Nature, feel the need for multiple or feminine models of the Sacred, find in ritual a source of nurturance and an outlet for creative self-expression. Those are the motivations that attract me to seekers.

But consider this: The motivations that sound best to you are likely to be those that drew you in your own time. Maybe that's as it should be. Similar motivations go a long way towards establishing the compatibility that allows us to work well together in a student-teacher relationship.

As a mentor, it is important to be very clear about which motivations you think are or are not appropriate. Understand and honor your own boundaries.

3. Able

When we reach the question of abilities, we are asking what gifts this seeker brings to our community. People are not inter-changeable parts. Each of us comes with a different combination of inborn talents and temperaments and with the experiences, knowledge, and skills developed throughout our lives.

I believe that those inborn talents and temperaments — gifts of the Gods — are also callings, potentials to be developed and placed at the service of the Gods, the people, and the Earth. Again, you must decide for yourself which tempera-ments and talents are essential, desirable, or irrelevant to your way of working. Here are some possibilities of desirable traits, just to start your own thought process. These lists can easily lengthen.

Temperaments
- Discretion
- Respect for others
- Honesty
- Reliability
- Generosity
- Patience

Talents
- Imagination and creativity
- Psychic or empathic sensitivity
- Critical thinking

- Verbal or other self-expression
- Ritual performance abilities (e.g., musicality)

There's another factor that affects ability: life circumstances. Is the seeker realistically able to commit to your training program at this point in their life? What are the competing demands of school or work? What are the family responsibilities? If they are a parent, what are the child care arrangements? If they are married or otherwise in a committed relationship, how does the mate feel about the time and energy demands of the work? Do they have a way of getting to group meetings? Do they have any health problems that would consistently interfere with full participation?

The practical questions can go on and on. It isn't that we're limiting ourselves to students who have no life problems or impediments — there would be no active Pagan renaissance if we all waited for that. Instead, ensure that any difficulties are being addressed, managed, and resolved, and that the seeker is indeed free to become an active and enthusiastic student.

A GOOD MATCH?

Admirable though they are, the virtues that make a person right for the Path are not rare. They are both widespread and fairly abstract. It's relatively easy to determine whether a seeker is, in general, right for the path.

In contrast, each individual mentor is different, even those in the same Tradition or lineage. Each of us has our own viewpoint, style, habits, and quirks. And seekers also have their personal quirks. So finding a good match between seeker and mentor can be a lot more complicated —in fact, quirky. Here is the central question: how will this particular seeker benefit from working with this particular mentor?

After that comes a whole bunch of nitty-gritty issues. A perfect fit is highly improbable. But the more compatible you are on these details, the more comfortably you will work together.

- *Learning/teaching style.* Does the seeker prefer a highly structured curriculum laid out by the teacher, or are they a self-directed learner? Is your teaching style directive or student-centered? If you have a structured curriculum, will it be covering the areas the seeker would like to learn more about?
- *Ritual style.* Does your worship tend to be more shamanic or ceremonial? Do you work from an inherited script, create your own, or work extemporaneously? Again, how does this mesh with the seeker's background and preferences?
- *Deity.* Are you and this seeker drawn to the same Deity or pantheon? If not, do you feel competent to guide a seeker who is working with different God/desses from yours?
- *Expectations.* What kinds of demands do you make of your students? How frequent and how long are your mentoring sessions? How much "homework" do you usually assign? Can this seeker participate fully while meeting other responsibilities and enjoying a well-balanced life?
- *Personal history.* How were each of you shaped by your original religious background and training? Are there incompatible hidden assumptions arising from very old religious patterns?

These are just some examples of the kinds of questions involved in matching seekers with mentors.

Take some time now to figure out what you are looking for in a seeker. Who would you enjoy working with and why? What are you looking for? What would you prefer to avoid?

When somebody seeks mentoring from you, find out all you can about them. Talk with them at length. If they have references, check them. Write out a summary of your findings; this will pull your impressions together. Do some structured divination about the probable success of the relationship and record the outcome.

Then set it all aside. Let it germinate in your deep mind for a while. Meditate, daydream, and sleep on this question. See what comes up. It is these internal responses, which perhaps carry the Sacred Wisdom within them, that should govern your tentative decision to accept, defer, refer, or reject any particular seeker.

Obviously, acceptance is what is sometimes called an *and-gate*. All the time you were checking out this seeker, they were checking you out. They may have also been conducting this exploratory process with several other mentors at the same time. Just as you may choose to refer them, they may choose to work with someone else. Just as you may choose to defer them, they may decide to postpone study until they finish graduate school, raise their baby, or complete chemotherapy. Just as you may choose to reject them, they may decide they don't want to pursue this path at all, or that they certainly do — with any mentor but you. And that is okay. By process of elimination, you will find the students whom you'll most enjoy mentoring. It's funny how those are also the ones you'll mentor best. Quality matters. Quantity doesn't matter at all.

In fact, nobody actually *needs* to serve as a mentor. To the extent that your own contact with the Entheoi is strong, that the awen is flowing well within you, you will certainly need to express that in some form of service and/or creativity. In fact, all healthy adults, religious or not, have an inner need for *generativity*, which means a need to serve the young and through them, help shape the future. It's also natural for you to want to earn the respect of other Pagans by doing good work. But mentoring is only one possible way of meeting these needs.

A STUDENT'S VIEW

Many thanks to Bell, a Wiccan elder and teacher in Winnipeg, for sharing her memories and thoughts about her process of entry into our community and her progress into elder status. The following is excerpted from our electronic correspondence.

JUDY: What do you think a new Pagan needs from community elders?

BELL: What they do NOT need is for the elders to be always and publicly available.

I am in favor of the newcomer having a threshold to climb, in order to enter deeper Craft. The Craft is not suited to all people. The qualities needed to climb the threshold should include attentiveness to signals smaller than a billboard, patience, persistence, and discernment.

It used to be that such persistence and attention was needed just to find books, much less teachers. Currently you can almost get a Wicca 101 book in with the Cornflakes — there is no threshold save literacy and a little cash.

That's not too bad a problem, since many people treat written stuff as fiction and don't seriously try to apply it. But for a living teacher to impart skills the person isn't ready for can be counterproductive.

Having said that, there needs to be some sort of availability. Elders have differing preferences as to how public they are, and how often. Being a baby elder, I still host Open Circles (completely open to the public) or community circles (open by word of mouth or invitation) once or twice a year. Older elders might attend such events, but wouldn't run them. *Really* old elders are often not visible as such, or even visible as practitioners.

Practicing Wicca, well, takes a lot of teaching and a lot of study. Considering this, I am surprised that so many people actually undertake it.

What appears to happen most often is that someone will pick up a couple of books, learn enough to become interested, and then begin climbing a staircase of teachers, so to speak — beginning with the most available and working up (if they progress) to less easily available and more challenging instructors. Three or four steps down, the teachers further up the stairs are not visible. But they are there.

A teacher reaching downwards to help the less experienced cannot do that job unless he/she is at the same time reaching upwards for help. If a teacher thinks he is at the top of the heap, the flow is broken and dries up rapidly.

JUDY: What do you think about individual spiritual development and personal mentoring for Pagan laity, before a person is ready to make a commitment to the Craft, or Druidry, or any of the other structured Traditions?

BELL: I can detail my entry into the Craft. In 1991 my friend Piper, a musician and artisan, mentioned that there would be a Wiccan open circle in the park, and I might find it interesting. Politely, I told him I would be washing my hair that night, but thanks anyway. Over subsequent months he continued to invite me, and one evening I joined a circle near the river. Though the ritual wasn't anything special — no fireworks, no golden clouds — I tasted something I had wanted all my life and thought I would never have. I borrowed some books, soon beginning to practice.

What elders aided me as I went along? (Elders being all those who knew more than I and were willing to help.)

First there were fellow practitioners, many only weeks ahead of me. These folks provided a forum for discussion. We talked the sun down and up again, I swear; we talked like college students discovering Wittgenstein. In talking and working with each other we established a common language: conceptual, verbal, and operational.

Shared concepts were fleshed out and became firm in the context of our discussions — also shared experiences. Take energy, for instance. Like the Christian experience of "the Spirit," it is real and unmistakable once a person is accustomed to it. But our culture disparages this sort of experience. Using energy in groups, and reframing the sensation we called "feeling the energy" as a real sensory input and not merely an underdone bit of potato, firmed up our wobbly control and made our workings effective.

Books — some better, some worse — filled my head for a couple of years. I began with Adler, went on to Starhawk and Cunningham, and sideways into Walker, Fitch, the Farrars, Valiente, and an awful lot of Goddess-related historical books which provided a vision of woman as holy, powerful, and wise — concepts I really needed at that time. Ideas have power, even if they are historically inaccurate. (This could be a motto for much of early Wicca, if Hutton is anything to judge by.)

Early on I had teaching from an elderly traditional practitioner (Alexandrian, I believe) who, over the years, taught quite a number of us unscrubbed pups, may her memory be blessed.

In addition, through solitary meditations and ceremonial practice, there was an infusion of spiritual teaching from the Gods themselves. Just sitting with a candle, in circle, in silence, receptive and trusting, was a powerful way to advance.

All this brought me, I would estimate, to a level of reliable apprentice-level practice. I began teaching, which thank heavens both my students and I survived. I ran a pagan bookstore for a couple of years, learning a lot and getting all the glitter knocked off my wand.

But then I entered another area of learning. I had reached a point where I wasn't moving forward. I ranged farther afield, gathering riches from other faith communities. Bless him, a Catholic priest took me under his wing and taught me elements of deeper meditation and prayer. I studied Sufi writings, Jewish and Christian mysticism, and interspersed it with a couple of forms of psychology. I got interested in Kabbalah — not the magical, but the mystical end of it. Through an astonishingly powerful Anglican church I made peace with the Christian faith, which I had left in adolescence because there was no nourishment for me there. Having made peace (I still read and love Merton and Eckhart), I learned that though I could now respect the Christian way, that path wasn't for me.

This brings us up to the present [January 8, 2002]. I have taken early retirement from a technical career. I've left electrical wiring behind, embracing poetry and painting and much more selective teaching of the Craft. And I am finally, after 11 years of solitary practice, working regularly with a sound, sane little group.

Bell's story really shows what the quest is like. Remember it as you read the rest of this book. I was particularly struck by how she found a variety of mentors along her path, each meeting the need she was feeling at a particular time.

Mentoring is a relationship in which an elder and a younger person work together towards the healthy growth of the younger. It can only work well when two appropriate and compatible people come together. The next chapter will look at some of the things they do, the actual techniques of mentoring.

NOTES

[1] For more information see M. Macha NightMare's book, *Witchcraft and the Web: Weaving Pagan Traditions Online* (Toronto: ECW Press, 2001).

[2] Polly Young-Eisendrath, "Psychotherapy as Ordinary Transcendence: The Unspeakable and the Unspoken," in *The Psychology of Mature Spirituality*, eds. Polly Young-Eisendrath and Melvin E. Miller (Philadelphia: Routledge, 2000), 133–44.

Safe Space

CHAPTER 3

NURTURING INTERACTIONS

IT STARTS WITH THE FIRST SEEKER. SOMEBODY HAS got to know you at some community activity, or maybe just through the grapevine. They feel that it's time they got more serious about their Pagan study and practice. They admire you, and think they might want to become more like you as they progress on the path. They ask whether you might give them some advice. Your deep inner voice says *Yes*. Another part of you might be terrified of the responsibility, feeling unskilled and unprepared, even unworthy. What now?

Sit with it. Think about all the questions and issues described in the last chapter. Discuss the possibility with your own elders, or with close and trusted friends. Dream and meditate, maybe do some divination. Let a week or two go by. If your deep inner voice is still saying *Yes*, maybe even a little bit louder, so be it — the answer is yes. What now?

Just how do you foster your friend's progress?

The same inner voice that said *Yes* will guide you. You can trust that. You will also most certainly learn from experience, although that prospect may not be reassuring. You can learn from the collective experience of other mentors, and from other kinds of helping professionals. This chapter will survey some of what I think Pagan mentors can learn from secular counselors and from spiritual directors of other religions.

Let's start by defining three related ways of helping people.

- *Counseling* is a process in which one person helps another to understand the kinds of problems and perplexities that occur in the course of normal life, and to make and implement good personal decisions.
- *Pastoral Counseling* is counseling within a religious context. The issues being examined may not be overtly religious, but both client and counselor intend to apply the values and teachings of the religion they share to the issues under consideration. The counselor is often a clergy member, and is expected to be expert in what that religion teaches.
- *Spiritual Mentoring* is a relationship in which an elder assists a seeker with their spiritual growth within a particular faith tradition. Mentoring has aspects of teaching, priesthood, coaching, and counseling. The focus is on spiritual and religious developmental issues, but other aspects of life may be addressed.

There's a great deal of overlap between these three approaches to helping. They call on many of the same personality traits and skills. All are based on the principle that people find their own answers with support — and sometimes guidance — from trained helpers. My own secular professional training is in counseling, so it's natural for me to start with the areas that mentoring and counseling have in common.

ACTIVE LISTENING

The core technique, the art of any of the "helping professions" is active listening. Active listening itself has three main components:
1. Listen.
2. Let them know you're listening.
3. Ground.

Just like the Wiccan Rede, this is the kind of profoundly true statement that I can say while standing on one foot — but will have to spend a long time figuring out how to apply to real life. So, let's slow it down.

1. Listen

Most of the time, most of us listen with only part of our attention. While the other person is still speaking, we are thinking about what we want to say next. Sometimes we are even thinking of something entirely unrelated . . . "add one cup sugar." When we are listening to emotionally intense material, as mentors often do, we can block the feelings behind a cold shield of "objectivity." We might also get so caught up in our own emotional reactions — how we would feel if we were in a similar situation, based on our own experiences — that we miss or ignore those of the speaker.

Instead of all that, we open ourselves to what our students are saying and respond to them with *empathy*.

The word *empathy* is actually a poor and misleading translation of the German word *einfuhlung*. A more direct and correct translation would be *in-feeling* or *feeling into something*.

Empathy is not something we have, not just passive receptivity to the student's perceptions and emotions. It's something we do, the active practice of feeling into the inner world of another: their perceptions, reactions, memories, hopes, fears, dreams — all that is sometimes called their *inscape*. As best we can, we set aside our own inscape to enter theirs, hoping thus to help their self-exploration. By the classic definition, this is an act of magic, of changing our own consciousness in accordance with will.

It is also a Sacred act of meditation on the Entheoi within the other person, and absolutely essential to the mentoring process. The student is working towards opening, maintaining, clarifying, and deepening their own conscious contact with the Entheoi. They will be reading books and dancing, building shrines and meditating, using many different resources and techniques in their spiritual quest.

The process of articulating for you what they tried and with what results helps them make sense of all these experiences for themselves. Your reverent attention to the Entheoi within your student helps your student become aware of indwelling Sacred Presence. Your active and empathic listening encourages your student's introspection. Your caring feedback helps them plan their next steps along the path.

When you sit with a student, the first challenge is to listen as openly as possible, without expectation or judgment. Always remember: this person is not you. No matter how similar to you they may seem, they've come through a substantially different set of formative experiences. The most powerful influence comes from previous religious experience. Race, class, gender, culture, region, specific family history, and specific personal history all also make a difference. You will hear your students better, and they will feel safer to speak, if you can set your theories aside and just listen.

The student needs somebody to just be there, listen, and accept what they are saying. They haven't always had that. Being free to speak even the most hurtful things, and feeling heard, understood, and accepted: this is what it means to feel safe. All their experience, from earliest childhood to the way you respond to them today, builds or destroys that sense of safety that is utterly necessary to further exploration.

You may be uncomfortable in the presence of grief, pain, anger, or confusion. Bear with it. Don't rush to shut them up with slick pieties or cheap comfort. That only cuts off their process. On the other hand, always assume that the student shared as much as they could in the moment. Don't press or pry. The student knows how much they can face right now, and how safe they feel, far better than you can.

Some of the student's message is verbal, some is nonverbal (tone of voice, facial expression, posture, and very much more). Some of the student's message is consciously chosen, some comes from their unconscious. You will receive some of it consciously, some of it subliminally. What you have received subliminally will also shape your reactions. If you really listen and really care, you will inevitably have emotional responses to what you hear.

Paradoxically, the second challenge is to listen as openly as possible to *yourself*. Your own inscape, though set aside, must not be completely hidden from you. It's important to distinguish emotions you are picking up from the student, and likely sharing with them, from those that are entirely your own. For example, while sitting with a very angry student, an empathic mentor would feel into that student's anger. But if the mentor had had previous painful experiences with anger, they might also be feeling some fear.

Learning to listen like that, actively and empathically, may seem daunting. In reality, your own meditation practice is the best possible preparation. By opening yourself to the Entheoi, you have learned to be open to your students and to the Entheoi within each one.

2. Let Them Know You're Listening

Listening is absolutely necessary for effective mentoring, but not sufficient. I could listen intently and openly — and invisibly — from the other side of a one-way mirror. That might well be instructive for me, but not helpful for the student.

Students need to *know* that somebody's hearing them, valuing them as human, supporting their quest. They can venture deeper, and face what they find, when they know they are not alone. The mentoring relationship offers them safe space, but not in the sense of a base camp to which they return periodically. It's more like a snug, brightly painted gypsy wagon that moves along with them, supplying shelter and sustenance along the path, extending their range, not restricting it.

The third challenge, then, is to respond with acceptance and encouragement. While open and active listening may be a spiritual practice, we let people know we're listening through a series of fairly simple skills (sometimes called *attending behavior*). Look at the person, lean forward, make eye contact, give the occasional encouraging nod. Respond appropriately. Here are some responses that help:

- **Summarizing** ("I want to be sure I understand what you have told me.")
- **Interchangeable responses**, especially those that are worded to reflect feelings and beliefs ("I hear you saying that you are frustrated by how difficult it is for you to remember your dreams.")
- **Invitations to clarify** ("Would you like to talk about it some more?" "Could you tell me more about your confusion?" "Could you give me another example of a time when you got that upset?" "Let's see if we can figure out the assumptions behind that point of view." "How do you think you might act upon that feeling?")
- **"I" messages** ("I am curious as to how you dealt with that difficult situation." "I am eager to know more about your thinking on this issue." "I am pleased to know that things worked out so well for you." "I am confused about what you are saying to me.")

- **Low-level inferences** ("It seems like you were really disappointed." "I have a hunch that it was very difficult for you to be assertive in this situation.")

In contrast, here are some other responses that tend to inhibit people, making effective inner work more difficult and less likely:

- **Put-downs** and personal criticisms ("If you are not keeping a daily journal, you are just being lazy or disorganized.")
- **Arguing** with viewpoints and beliefs ("Your interpretation of that dream makes no sense at all.")
- **Rejection of feelings** ("You know that endings are part of the Cycle. You have no right to resent them, let alone to get angry with the Gods!")
- **Giving orders** ("Look, it's really very simple, what you need to do is . . .")
- **Patronizing the student** ("Lots of people get mixed up about that. It's normal — don't worry about it.")
- **Lecturing or moralizing** ("When I was new to the path . . .")

Most often, after listening as openly as possible, the best response is simply to reflect back to the student what you have heard. This is called reflective, passive, or *resonant* empathy. A model commonly given to counseling students is, "Gerald, I hear you saying you are feeling _____ about _____." (Don't worry, you'll find more natural wordings.)

Such easy and comforting responses belong in the early phases of the exploration, while the student is getting used to working with you, and possibly to the path itself. You'll also use reflective responses whenever the student is assimilating some new inner discovery, or if you sense that the student is getting stressed or upset. Gentle pacing helps maintain the student's sense of safety, without which no real work can take place.

Since nonverbal communication is often also unconsciously sent, you may become aware of some reactions or even learnings that are not yet consciously available to the student. As the student becomes more comfortable with you and with their own inner exploration, you may occasionally want to use a more active form of empathic response, sometimes called *additive* or *imaginative* empathy. In these responses, you will be describing your perceptions of the client's nonverbal communication. The model is, "Doreen, I hear you saying you are feeling _____ about _____. I am also sensing _____." *Additive empathy does not mean adding to the student's feelings; it means adding to their conscious knowledge of feelings they were already having inside.*

Be sure to present any additive responses very, very tentatively. Always remember that you might be mistaken. You are still likely to be viewing a student's inscape through the lens of your own, and that might distort their message. No one can perfectly distinguish perceptions from inferences from projections. Leave room for them to correct you. Explaining exactly how you were off-base is an excellent way for them to get to the heart of the matter. Encourage this.

If you insist that you know more about a student's life than they do, you will erode their sense of safety. They may shut down. Worse yet, they may start telling you what you want to hear. Worst of all — especially if they think of you as an authority figure — they might suppose that you know better than they do about their own experiences, perceptions, and feelings. If things deteriorate that far, their inscape becomes less accessible not only to you, but to them. Then you haven't just failed to help, you've actively done harm. Instead, realize that for this work, you are a helper and not a leader. Make your suggestions, but let them steer.

3. Ground

As a mentor, you will hear about a lot of stress, pain, and grief. In offering the other person the comfort of being heard, in opening yourself to them, you are also absorbing energies that nobody needs to retain.

You deserve to take care of yourself, and if you're serious about being around for the long haul, you *need* to take care of yourself. Do whatever you need to do after each mentoring session to let the energy go, clearing the slate for whatever comes next. Do whatever works for you: bathe in salt water, hug a tree, play tennis.

DEVELOPING EMPATHY

Allowing another into our inscape is an act of great trust. Entering the inscape of another is an awesome privilege and responsibility. No one is ever perfectly "ready" for such deep contact.

Please, as you do this, have reasonable expectations of yourself. It's important to understand that empathy is not an inborn talent but a practice, and, in time, a trained skill. It's also an ideal, a model, a goal we work towards but never completely achieve. For one thing, our capacity varies with what's happening in our own lives. It's harder to open to another when you are tired, scared, hurting. Also, even at our best moments, our own inscapes still shape and color our perceptions.

The practice of empathy, then, requires us to explore our own inscapes, develop our own insights, create the inner clarity that makes real listening possible. This deep self-exploration will bring us to our own hard, frightening, and painful moments. Sometimes we will recall ugly memories or face, name, and integrate the parts of our own hearts and minds that we were taught by example to reject. Neither is it easy to identify and take responsibility for our strengths.

Be careful not to push yourself too hard or too fast. Be as gentle and respectful — and as thorough — with yourself as you would be with one of your students. Remember that this process is not altogether new to you, and you already have some good tools. Self-exploration is an important component of any spiritual practice. Awareness meditation helps, as does dream exploration and journal work. And you may want to get some individual help from someone you trust who has preceded you on this path.

This is the Goddess's on-the-job training program: you do the best you can. You keep working to deepen and clarify your own insight. You stretch your skills, but do not go beyond them. You keep track of how your clients do. You find an elder to talk things over with. And, above all, you acknowledge your mistakes so you may learn from them.

Empathy is an intellectual, emotional, and, ultimately, a spiritual discipline. Like all others, it requires consistent and patient practice. Practice helps us to listen openly at the times when it isn't easy. Insight helps us distinguish our "stuff" from others'. Be patient with yourself. Give yourself room and time to grow.

PRIVACY

Spiritual growth can come hard. Old hurts and old habits block the way. The work may involve facing painful memories, long buried. It may require the sacrifice of major components of the student's self-image, and significant behavioral risk-taking. It almost certainly involves the special openness of trance states.

Those who experiment with themselves are vulnerable. Few would risk such deep self-exploration if their discoveries seemed likely to become common gossip. Secular counselors recognize this, as do the clergy of religions that require individual confessions.

Safe space is private space. So a mentoring session must be like a cast Circle: whatever is said or done within should normally not be discussed with anyone who was not present. Students deserve and need assurance of privacy, especially in a community as small as ours. Pagans live in a fishbowl.

Nothing in nature is so very pure. Although keeping secrets is a way of life for us, we need to understand both the practical risks and the ethical limits of secrecy. Sometimes life presents us with hard and tragic choices. Thinking about the issues involved *before* you find yourself in a crisis situation can be a valuable preparation.

The risks are legal. The mentoring role is arguably a clergy role, but may not be recognized as such in every jurisdiction. Even if it is, that doesn't guarantee our safety. We'd like to think that as clergy, our communications with those who seek our counsel are legally protected, "privileged" communications. We'd like to believe that our religious status safeguards us, at least from the threat of jail. But it's not that simple.

In 1994, the members of Iron Oak Coven in Florida faced a different freedom of religion issue. They fought and won their case, yes, but had to take a second mortgage on their house to pay their lawyer. What about those of us who have no house to mort-gage? Our legal rights are only made real when we have the resources and the determination to defend them.

Beyond that, the legal right of *any* clergy to remain silent varies from state to state and with the type of case. Many states, for example, mandate the reporting of child abuse. In 1984, also in Florida, a fundamentalist Christian minister, Rev. John Mellish, counseled a child abuser in his congregation. The man subse-quently confessed, pled guilty, and still the court demanded the pastor's testimony. Pastor Mellish refused on principle, and went to jail for contempt of court, setting an honorable example for all clergy of all religions. Understand that where the law denies the privilege of confidential communication to anybody, Pagan mentors cannot claim religious discrimination.

Each of us needs to research what the law actually is where we live in order to assess our risks and protect ourselves as best we can. No protection is perfect. Living by our values is not always comfortable or profitable or even safe, but it is the meaning of the word *religion*.

The risks are legal and practical, but the limits are ethical. There are a very few heartbreaking circumstances in which keeping silence does more harm than breaking it. For those of us who live by the Wiccan Rede, these are moments of tragic conflict.

The secular counseling profession has its own strong tradition of confidentiality. But professional counselors acknowledge clear limits to that confidentiality, and good reasons for those limits. We can learn from this example. In the early 1970s, Tatiana Tarasoff was a student at the University of California. Another student, obsessed with thoughts of murdering her, sought help at the university counseling center. The counselor kept silence. Tatiana, unwarned, was later murdered. Her parents won a wrongful death suit. The California Supreme Court upheld the decision on appeal (*Tarasoff v. Regents of the University of California*, 1976) and so established a legal "duty to warn" in situations of serious danger to self or others.

Don't think that our spiritual orientation protects us from dangerous fanaticism. It may actually increase our risk. Terrorists who conduct suicide missions believe themselves to be consecrated martyrs obeying God's holy will. Think: what would you do if your student told you that their inner voice had commanded them to shoot abortionists or send letter bombs to polluters . . . or to take their son up a mountain and stab the boy to death?

Very rarely, a crisis may arise that is truly beyond our ability to handle within the community. At such times, secular law commands us to get whatever outside help is needed: a doctor, a firefighter, a police officer. Silence then could leave us legally liable, but that alone is not a good reason to violate a confidence. When there is truly imminent, serious danger, the Rede gives us that reason.

The Limits of Confidentiality

There are times when it is appropriate, or even necessary, to reveal information that was entrusted to us as mentors. Here are some clear instances:

- Your student presents an imminent, serious danger to self or others.
- Your student requests that you release information to others.
- Another person is present in the room, clearly visible to your student (and, most often, at your student's request).

Here are some borderline situations (you should discuss these with your students before you share their story with others):

- You feel the need to get advice from your own elder or from some other kind of expert, perhaps a psychologist.
- You are in a mentors' support group and want to discuss your student's issues and progress with your colleagues there.
- You normally discuss religious concerns with your working partner.

Finally, you may someday find yourself under legal pressure to break confidence. It's very important that you become familiar with applicable law where you live before any problems arise. In situations like these, you must weigh all possible legal and moral consequences and make your best conscientious decision:

- A court orders release of information.
- Your student is a legal minor, and their parents demand disclosure.
- It is a "mandated reporter" situation, which varies from jurisdiction to jurisdiction. These may include child abuse, suicide risk, drug use, or other problems.

I strongly suggest that you ponder these situations, and any others that you can recall or imagine, before they arise. How do you think you would respond to them? As you understand your own reactions, you can let your students know what your limits are. This allows them to decide how much personal information they can comfortably share with you.

As a rule, before sharing anyone else's personal story, *always ask first!*

THE HOLDING ENVIRONMENT

Active listening, empathy, and privacy are three main principles that mentoring holds in common with other helping professions such as counseling. All three work together to help the student feel safe in thinking and talking about the deeply personal issues of spirituality with a mentor. The metaphor *safe space* has come up before in this chapter. A more formal, and more specific, term for safe space is *holding environment*.[1] This concept is very relevant and useful for Pagan mentors. An effective holding environment performs three critical functions:

1. *Holding on*: warmth, validation, unconditional positive regard, support, *agape* — these are many different terms for the same thing. This is your clearly communicated belief that your student is a good and worthy and capable person with every right to travel the path (and if you don't genuinely believe

this, you should certainly not be mentoring them). We call this love.

It's important also to let students know that they are not alone. Part of a mentor's teaching function is to validate and contextualize the student's Sacred experiences. Others — including you — have traveled this path before, encountered and overcome similar obstacles, even made the same dumb mistakes, and were able to keep going.

2. *Letting go*: respect and challenge your willingness to back off and let your student attempt difficult and risky activities, sometimes even to fail and learn the lessons of those failures; encouragement rather than protectiveness. This is your clearly communicated belief that your students have the capacity to find Sacred guidance from within and to make and implement good decisions in their lives. We call this trust.

A beginner may be temporarily dependent on their mentor. Often they will weave a fantasy in which the mentor's love and trust are perfect beyond reasonable human possibility. Mentors may temporarily accept this projection and this dependency so the student can feel safe enough to risk growing into their own confident autonomy. A good mentor works towards resolving this dependency and transforming it into self-reliance and reliance on the Entheoi as soon as possible.

It can be difficult and challenging for the mentor to let go. Many of us were originally drawn to mentoring roles, or to the helping professions, by our own need to be needed. This need often arises from childhood insecurities. It can degenerate into codependency. A codependent person uses excessive involvement with the problems of other people as a way to avoid facing their own problems.

Mentors who are extremely codependent sometimes even hamper or block their students' development. By keeping their students artificially needy, needy mentors can continue to feel needed and important. To manipulate students in this manner is a complete betrayal of the mentor's calling.

3. *Sticking around*: being there to help the student recover and rethink when they've run into a roadblock, check on progress, learn from any mistakes, plan for the next stretch of the path. We call this commitment. Commitment anchors love and trust in truth.

Mentoring relationships go through active and inactive phases. There can even be some long, angry separations as students break through dependency. But authentic mentoring relationships only end with fulfillment. Even a dead mentor may stick around in the student's memories, becoming an on-going source of guidance and inspiration, one of the student's Mighty Dead. When the student catches up with the mentor, they become equal companions and friends on the path. Mentoring is over then, but a friend sticks around for you.

Spiritual mentoring shares a lot of theory and technique with secular counseling. The difference is the explicitly spiritual focus and goal. In accordance with that spiritual focus, mentoring sessions often include explicitly spiritual practices. Knowing that the Entheoi are ever present, we turn our awareness towards Them and welcome Their participation in our work.

Please notice that each of the three functions of a holding environment derives from an inner attitude of the mentor: love, trust, and commitment. From a Pagan perspective, then, all three grow from willed changes of consciousness, from magic. We can, and as mentors we do, choose those ways of being with our students. As magic users understand empathy, it can send out emotional states as well as take them in. By projecting our love, trust, and commitment, we create the holding environment, the safe space that supports our students' growth.

Will is made manifest by skill. Consciousness is not changed by wishful thinking, but by practiced technique. Here are some things you can do to help attune yourself to the energies of love, trust, and commitment; create a warm, nurturing, and specifically Pagan space; and draw on the energies of the Ancient Gods:

- Set the session time apart from other concerns or activities. Conduct your normal mentoring sessions by appointment. Start on time. Close gently, but approximately on time. As much as you can, prevent interruptions. Turn off the ringer on your telephone. Do everything you can to signal your student that this time is theirs. (Note: spiritual emergency supersedes all time boundaries, even if the person shows up at your door in crisis at 3 AM.)

- Prepare and consecrate the space. If possible, use a room that has a door you can close. Make sure the temperature and lighting are comfortable. Keep this space clean and orderly; clutter distracts. Simple house cleaning, done with focused intent, is a powerful act of preparatory magic for mentoring or for ritual.

- Set up a small, simple shrine to represent the Sacred Presence: a plant or some flowers, perhaps a statue, a candle. Cense and asperge the room in preparation for a session.

- Prepare yourself. Rest and meditate before a session. Reflect and journal after, and invite your student to do the same. If your meetings are widely spaced — and once a month is fairly normal — you can each review your journal to prepare for a session.

- Formally open each session. This should be something very simple, like lighting the candle or speaking a short invocation. If you prefer to open and close more elaborately, lengthen the session time to allow for it.
- Start each session with a short period of meditative silence. Do not hesitate to take additional silent time during a session as well, so each of you can seek inner wisdom. Remember, it's really a three-way interaction.
- Don't rush to fill a silence. The student may be reaching deep inside, trying to find words for subtle experience. Be alert for nonverbal communication and receptive to your own inner voice during silent moments. But if the student really seem stuck, use open-ended questions like, "How is it with you right now?" or "What seems to be nurturing or hindering you today?"
- Remember that conversation is important, but not your only option. You may also sometimes choose to chant together, do a guided meditation or some other sort of exercise, share some ritual practice.
- Suggest, perhaps, some practice for your student to do at home between sessions, or recommend something for them to read. If you have done this, ask how it worked or what they learned.
- Formally close each session. Ask the student for a short summary. Take a few minutes for silent reflection. Offer brief thanks to the Entheoi for being present. If you have lit a candle, extinguish it.
- Offer the student a light snack or beverage to help them fully ground before they leave, particularly if the session involved any trance work.
- Take time to fully ground, rest, and refresh yourself when the student has left. Do not schedule mentoring sessions back to

back. Allow at least as much time for self-renewal between sessions as you do for each session.

- Most of us do this kind of work for love alone while supporting ourselves with a day job. If that's your situation, make sure you allow time to eat and relax after you get home from work before starting a session. Don't try to schedule more than one mentoring session in an evening. If at all possible, don't schedule them on two nights in a row.

All of the above is lovely, and helpful. Do it if you can. But don't become dependent on any of it. None of it is absolutely necessary. Not one bit. I've done effective mentoring on a park bench or in a fast-food hamburger joint, and so has anybody else who's been doing this work for any length of time. What you truly need — does this sound familiar? — can be found inside yourself.

Remember, imagine, enter into the heart space from which you mentor, and draw your dear student in. Feel that? Project it. What you do inside yourself changes the emotional atmosphere around you. You, mentor, are the heart of the holding environment, the creator of the safe space. If you need to, you can do the essential magic anytime, anywhere.

CONFRONTATION: TOUGH LOVE

As you work with students, you'll begin to notice instances when they tell you one thing but show you something quite different. They are not lying; a lie is an *intentional* false statement. Instead, they are relating their honest, but inaccurate, self-perception. Eventually the time comes to tell the student about an apparent inconsistency that you've noticed. This is what helpers mean by the word *confrontation*.

When somebody tells you they've had a confrontation, do you think about a tense, angry argument or possibly even a brawl?

Most people do. Even my trusty *American Heritage Dictionary* tells me that *confront* means "to come face to face with, especially with defiance or hostility." In radical contrast, my old counseling textbooks refer to *confrontation* as "an act of grace" or "a true act of caring." This is one of those annoying times when a specialized, professional use of a word is nearly opposite to the way people normally use it. Still, the concept of "appropriate" or "loving" confrontation is critical to our work as mentors.

Feelings can be elusive. Sometimes there are things about ourselves that we don't yet understand or even have hidden from ourselves, shadow areas inside that give rise to apparently inconsistent behavior. These holes in the student's self-awareness are also obstructions in the inner channel, obstacles on the path. If they can't access their own true feelings, how can they reach all the way in to the Entheoi?

Confrontation is an invitation to explore our inconsistencies and an opportunity to resolve them, and so it is a fast track to better self-knowledge and internal communication. It's hard to do, harder to do right, and very hard to accept. Here are some things to think about.

Timing is critical. Effective confrontation can only happen after the mentor and student have had a chance to get to know each other.

As a mentor, you know that first impressions are often off-base and almost always superficial. It takes some time to feel into another person's experience, and even more time to sense when they are ready to face and work through their more difficult issues.

Students need some time to size up whether the mentor is competent, caring, and honest. It takes time to build trust, but only trust can allow people to accept and integrate information that might be frightening, even painful.

There are two main circumstances in which mentors might offer confrontation, two very different kinds of inconsistencies: those between what we say and how we feel, and those between what we say and what we do.

Sometimes a person tells you they feel a particular way, but their voice, facial expression, posture, and your empathic sense all seem to reveal different emotions. If you feel the person is ready to take another step in self-understanding, you might choose to tell them what you've noticed, and what you think it might mean. Again, this is *additive* or *imaginative* empathy. If you offer additive empathy, remember to be sure to own your infer-ences, present them tentatively, and gracefully accept correction from the student. Your role is to invite self-exploration, not to compel it.

Other times, a person tells you they want or believe one thing, but their behavior seems unlikely to bring them to that goal, or is inconsistent with those beliefs. For example, they say they want to learn trance drumming, but never seem to find time to practice. They don't seem to you to be walking their talk. Again, confrontation means telling them about the inconsistency that you perceive, as caringly and as gently as possible.

Here are some sensible guidelines for confronting inconsistent behavior:

- Pick a calm and grounded moment for both of you within the safe, set-apart time and space of your mentoring session.
- Speak gently.
- Use "I" statements.
- Only address one or two key areas at a time. More than this is more than anyone can process at once.
- Only discuss things the person realistically could change. Be as specific as you can about how the behavior is conflicting

with the person's stated beliefs or interfering with progress towards their stated goals.

- Check that communication was clear. Have the person restate what you said if possible. Allow time for discussion of what you have presented. Be prepared to handle a defensive or angry initial reaction.

Be as firm as stone and as patient as a tree.

Never confront a student unless you are willing to deepen your involvement with them. Normally, offering loving confrontation means volunteering to stick around, to be there with the person as they work through the implications of the inconsistency with which you've presented them. It means volunteering to be even more of a mentor to them than you were before. Sadly, it doesn't always work out that way.

In a secular counseling situation, the goal is entirely the client's to determine. To resolve an inconsistency, the client can either adjust their behavior so that it will be more likely that they will achieve the goal, or decide that they were mistaken when they identified this goal. The counselor's job is to help them resolve the inconsistency in any way they choose. The outcome usually doesn't affect the counseling relationship.

For a Pagan mentor, the situation is quite different. The goal — the student's spiritual growth in a Pagan context — is the whole purpose of the student/mentor relationship. The student may decide that Paganism is not their true path. Even if it is, they may decide that they can't do advanced training justice while coping with other responsibilities or pursuing other dreams. This is their right and their choice, but it means that for now your active role as their mentor is irrelevant and will be ending.

If possible, have one last session in which you sum up what the relationship accomplished and draw closure. Give them your blessing and part in peace, trusting the Entheoi to guide them further. Although you won't be there to help with the next stretch of their journey, there are other helpers and other good paths.

ROLE CONFLICT

Structured Traditions, such as British Traditional Witchcraft, typically combine advanced spiritual development with training for their priesthood. A strong desire to serve in some way is a natural — I'd say inevitable — fulfillment of the spiritual quest. Priestly service is just one possibility. Others find outlets for the awen they've received in the arts, scholarship, social service . . . or even in mentoring other seekers. On the other hand, clergy who have not developed their own Sacred Contact are a travesty — uninspired plodders who know little more than rote repetition of clichés, rules, and rites, and who similarly limit their own students.

If your Tradition works on the assumption that all successful students will in time become priest/esses, take care to screen your candidates for that particular set of temperaments and talents. If you've done that, there's no reason why clergy training and spiritual development can't go on at the same time. Seminary students often work individually with spiritual directors while attending classes taught by other faculty.

However, in our small groups and in our apprenticeship-style training, students tend to have just one instructor at a time. If you're a group leader, you're probably both facilitating your students' spiritual development and evaluating them for their next degree. This is an inherent conflict of roles that may well lead to serious problems. Thinking about the issues involved before you find yourself in a crisis situation can be a valuable preparation.

The secular counseling profession is seriously concerned about multiple role relationships, relationships in which the two parties are something else to each other besides counselor and client. Although a consensus is not yet formed, most writers seem to feel that such relationships are always dangerous and usually harmful. So counselors are widely advised to avoid *any* other kind of relationship — professional or social — with their clients. That means they don't offer counseling to their barber.

That may work for people who are counselors *first*, and who live in metropolitan areas. But somewhere today, a student talked with a trusted schoolteacher about the problems at home. Somewhere else a doctor sat with a patient through his first reactions to a difficult diagnosis. Meanwhile, a divorce lawyer helped a client understand what she wants and what she can reasonably expect. As long as people have emotional reactions to their practical affairs, the professionals they turn to will always do "a little counseling on the side." The formal term for this is *ancillary counseling*. If teachers, doctors, and lawyers do ancillary counseling, clergy do very much more of it.

Counselors in small towns and rural areas, or in small, self-contained communities like military bases, also find it impossible to avoid all other contact with their clients. The same applies to Pagan counselors and mentors. Our community is small and relatively close-knit, which means that we are likely to encounter the same people in a variety of roles. You may be submitting your poetry to a magazine your student edits. Both of you may rehearse with the same chorus, or help out on the same park clean-up project. You'll probably be at some of the same gatherings or at open community Sabbat celebrations.[2]

It's not feasible for us to completely avoid multiple role relationships. Accepting that fact, we should also accept the responsibility of understanding the risks and learning how to manage the complexities involved. Multiple roles increase the risk of role conflict; they do not make role conflict inevitable.

A mentor is a hybrid of coach, counselor, priest/ess, and teacher, but those are all aspects of your service to your student. They can easily harmonize because they serve the same recipient in different ways. Let's call them a *role cluster*. A very different role cluster is required of those who train our future clergy: gatekeeper, evaluator, certifier. The two role clusters may conflict with each other because they are serving different people's needs, needs that can sometimes be opposed.

The structured Traditions generally have degree systems. The definition and even the sheer number of these degrees varies. But in each Tradition, some specified degree also conveys the legitimate right to train and initiate others. When you grant that particular degree, you are vouching to that person's future students, and to the community as a whole, that they have the competence, wisdom, and skill to serve as clergy. Mentors who have formed deep bonds with students will be tempted to gloss over problems rather than deny a friend's heartfelt desire to serve and be recognized. Instead, you must set aside the kindly instincts of a nurturer to become a judge.

Nobody feels safe while being judged. In order to benefit from your mentoring, a seeker needs to be completely open with you about their inner experience, including their confusions, doubts, and fears. Without active, empathic, nonjudgmental listening, how can the student feel safe about revealing these difficulties? Seekers who know they are being judged will be tempted to tell their mentors whatever they think the mentors want to hear.

Mentoring your barber is not a role conflict, but this is. A mentor serves the individual seeker. A judge serves the community. It's questionable whether the same person can effectively mentor and judge. But this is what the structured Traditions expect of their elder priesthood. What can we do? Here are some suggestions:

- Discuss the dangers of role conflict with any seeker while you are still considering working together before you actually start. Stay alert for any potential conflicts, and talk openly about these perceptions.
- Have clear standards and requirements for each degree. If possible, form these in discussion with other elders of your Tradition — with your own direct elders at least. Be sure the student understands exactly what these standards are.
- If possible, ask another closely related elder of the same Tradition whose judgment you respect to make the final assessment before granting any degree. If this is not an option, at least seek consultation with other elders who have not been directly mentoring this student.

The student made an appointment. They've arrived. You've taken their coat and brewed them a cup of tea. The two of you are sitting in not-quite comfortable silence in a comfortable room. It's time to start. Don't try right now to remember everything you've read in this chapter. You can't dance gracefully while watching your feet. You read it. You slept on it. It's there in your deep mind. Deeper yet in your mind is the guidance of the Entheoi. Dedicate this time to Their service and invite Their aid. Relax. Breathe deeply. Start. May the Ancient Ones bless your work!

TO LEARN MORE

Kennedy, Eugene and Sara C. Charles. *On Becoming a Counselor: A Basic Guide for Nonprofessional Counselors.* New York: Crossroads, 2001. ISBN 0824519132

This excellent book is written specifically for doctors, teachers, clergy, and others who need to deal with emotional issues in the course of practicing some other profession than counseling, and is therefore very useful for mentors.

NOTES

[1] Mary Baird Carlsen, *Meaning-Making: Therapeutic Processes in Adult Development* (New York: Norton, 1988), 51.

[2] My thanks to Ellen Friedman for pointing out this reality. For a full discussion, see her excellent article "Psychotherapist and Wiccan Clergy: The Ethics of a Dual Relationship," first published in *The Pomegranate* 14 (Nov. 2000), 16–25, and now available on the Proteus Coven Web site, <www.draknet.com/proteus/Ellen.htm>.

Road Maps

CHAPTER 4

MODELS OF MATURITY

EVERY PATH HAS ITS LANDMARKS, BUT DIFFERENT landmarks are salient for different people. A geologist, giving directions, might refer to particularly interesting rock outcrops along the way. An architect would have noticed distinctive buildings instead. Hikers and bicyclists are far more aware of the road's slope than motorists need to be. All these people have traveled the same road, but they experienced it — and will report on it — very differently. Any one of them could get confused by the directions another would give.

Inner paths are no different.

Even if there were just one spiritual path, different travelers would notice different landmarks along the way. But there are also many paths. Neo-Paganism itself is not one single path but a cluster of related ones, often within shouting distance of each other, sometimes combining for a stretch, but then wending off again on different trails. Other religions, too, have their multiplicities of sects, movements, and orders, so it's probably the same for them.

Let me emphasize this: There is no single true, or even best, neo-Pagan spiritual path. There is no single right way to describe *any* spiritual path. All maps are abstractions — and the inner realms are only subjectively knowable at that. Nobody can hand you a definitive map. Any such claim is bogus, particularly when made about Paganism. Ours is not a "one size fits all" religion, thank the Many Gods!

It took me an embarrassingly long time to figure this out.

About ten years ago, I read an article in which the author drew parallels between the theologies of four different religions and their members' perceptions of mature adult behavior.[1] It struck me that if there were characteristically Christian, Confucianist, Jewish, and Muslim notions of maturity, there might be a Pagan one as well.

That information would be really useful to Pagans who mentor or teach others. If we could articulate our collective notion of what a religiously mature lay Pagan is like, we could then ask ourselves what additional things we would look for before admitting someone to a training program, initiating them into one of our dedicated orders, or empowering them to train and initiate others. So I started asking other Pagan elders these questions, seeking consensus.

It seems, however, that we can't draw one map of Pagan spiritual development that works for all of us — at least not yet, and maybe never. Each elder seems to cherish their own personal sense of what the significant landmarks are along the path they follow. They want to work with students who will stop of their own accord to wonder at the same spots. Maybe that's another way to conceive of mentor/student compatibility.

Our polytheism further complicates the quest. Many Gods bless many paths in life. Behavior that is appropriate for a worshipper of Artemis might not be for a priestess of Aphrodite. In both classical Paganism and indigenous Pagan ways, it's normal for a person to follow and serve one particular member of the culture's pantheon. Santeros refer to that Deity as "the God on your head," and place great importance on discerning which one that is for each new initiate.

So there are more questions for us as we try to map this territory: What general core values do we all have in common, and what behaviors flow from those? How much do I need to know about a Deity in order to be a good mentor for that Deity's followers? What do I need to bear in mind when working with a person for whom a different God/dess is focal? How is it for the person, like me, who follows different Deities at different life phases?

That being said, there are also some features so major that just about every traveler will notice them: the Hudson River, the Statue of Liberty, the shape of the shoreline. These serve as points of reference for everybody's personal landmarks, basic understandings that we hold in common

Each of us draws our own map, the record of a lifetime's exploration. Map-makers start with bunches of information. They may have an older map, which they are updating to show changes in the land use. They may have surveyors' measurements, county property records, or aerial photos. They probably have some observations of their own. They will pick out the information that serves their purpose — some maps show roads, others show weather patterns — correlate the data, and draw the map.

In this chapter, I'll be sharing some interesting theories about stages of adult development in secular psychology and in non-Pagan religious studies. I think these are good resources for us. Of course, outsiders' overviews can't show the particulars of the Pagan paths. Still, they can give us some points of reference, the general outlines of the territory, a framework within which to place ourselves.

If any of these theories fascinate you, read the original writer for more detail and more depth. If they irritate you, reach inside yourself and ask why. Figuring out what exactly bothers you and why will help identify what does make sense to you. Best of all, you can choose the parts of all these systems that work best for you and create your own synthesis, consonant with your own experience and values.

If you're working within a Tradition or lineage, you have probably also inherited a sketch map from your elders, reflecting their collective observations. My suggestion: compare these Tradition-specific maps with the generic ones and adjust the accuracy of their general outlines. Academic psychologists and religious studies scholars have far better research tools and techniques for exploring the general lay of the land. Traditional maps fill in the details, leading you to this particular rock face to climb and that particular hot spring to bathe in, so you build a strong base of shared experience with your close kin.

Neither academic nor religious authority figures can relieve you of the obligation to think and contribute. The only way to truly make any system of thought or practice your own is to adapt it to your own core values, your own observations, your own working style. Rote repetition is not devotion — it's intellectual and spiritual laziness. Your own experience, not mine or anyone else's, should be your standard. Nothing less is authentic, and religion demands nothing less than authenticity.

Remember, our knowledge is incomplete. We are still rediscovering and reconstructing a path that was long neglected. Your open-minded observations and your creative contributions are genuinely needed in this effort. Knowledge shared is knowledge multiplied.

As you walk the path yourself and guide others, keep observing and learning. Think about what you and your students experience. Keep developing the path, clearing the overgrown spots and rebuilding the washouts. Keep updating, adapting, and annotating the map. Share what you learn with all who have the right to know, and learn from what they share with you. Together, we will rediscover all that was lost, rebuild all that was destroyed. Then we will continue discovering and creating from the point where our predecessors were forced to stop.

Here are four ways of understanding adult development, imported resources that I find particularly useful.

ERIKSON'S LIFE STAGES

Sigmund Freud, the founder of psychoanalysis, identified a series of childhood developmental stages. Erik Erikson (1902–1994) was a Freudian-trained psychoanalyst. In a sort of friendly amendment of Freud's theories, Erikson redefined the preadolescent stages and extended the notion of staged development through the whole of life.[2]

Erikson's stages are inevitable and time-specific. Both our bodies and our social roles change with age. Each life stage presents a challenge, a central conflict, which we must meet whether we are ready for it or not. Each age-related challenge offers us two choices, one clearly healthier than the other. So if we get it right, we are well prepared to move on to the next stage. If not, residual problems may hinder us through all the stages to come. Or we can work through the missed developmental step with much greater difficulty, perhaps in therapy.

A Simplified Form of Erikson's Model

Approximate Age	Major Conflict	Potential Virtue	Comments
0–1 baby	trust or mistrust	hope	infant is completely dependent on caregiver
2–3 toddler	autonomy or shame and doubt	will	learning to control the body
4–5 "play age"	initiative or guilt	purpose	learning to play with others
6–12 "school age"	industry or inferiority	competence	learning to work at structured tasks
13–18 adolescence	identity or confusion	fidelity	forming independent identity

19–25	intimacy or isolation	love	finding a mate
25–65	generativity or self-absorption and stagnation	care	contributing to the future
65+	integrity or despair	wisdom	adapting to limits, facing death

Pagan mentors normally work with adults, so the four preteen stages are not our immediate concern. Still, it's obvious that anyone who still has problems with basic trust, body control, social interaction, or focused activity is not ready for advanced spiritual development. That's one more way to assess potential students. (See Chapter 2 for more information on choosing students.)

Let's take a more detailed look at the four later stages:

- *Stage 4: Identity or Confusion.* In the teen years, people contend with the hormone storms of adolescence while separating from their parents, discovering their own values and beliefs, surveying career possibilities, and determining their sexual orientation. By doing all this, they develop a sense of personal identity.

  Teen seekers may just be exploring alternative religious paths as a way to detach themselves from their parents rather than responding to an inner calling. In any case, they are *exploring* religion along with all other areas of their lives. Commitments are made in the next stage. Esoteric development should follow exoteric commitment and stable practice.

  Some Pagan mentors will feel called to act as resources and guides for teens who are curious about Pagan lifeways. Although it's entirely praiseworthy to help kids work through their identity crises, don't confuse this precursor stage with advanced inner spiritual and magical growth.

- *Stage 5: Intimacy or Isolation.* In their early twenties, people typically find and commit to a lifemate. Erikson argues that a person without a strong sense of personal identity developed in the previous stage has nothing substantial to offer to a lover or spouse. Nor to the Gods or our community, I would add.
- *Stage 6: Generativity or Self-absorption and Stagnation.* In mature adulthood and middle age, people nurture and guide the next generation, and thus influence the future. Some of us do this with our own children, others by teaching in the classroom or on the job, and still others as elders in various religious communities.
- *Stage 7: Integrity or Despair.* Old age is a time for taking stock, for dealing with decreases in physical and even mental capacity, for drawing closure and approaching death. Those who have met the previous challenges well can look back with contentment and forward with serenity.

Erikson's model is quite important in the history of psychology. Just about every subsequent theory of adult development either refers or reacts to his. How useful is it for Pagan elders?

Notice that these are normal life stages. Most are universal and involuntary, none are the result of any intentional inner quest or spiritual path. Everyone who lives long enough will encounter these challenges regardless of which religion, if any, they practice.

People who are religiously affiliated, but not drawn to intense practice or advanced inner work, often seek guidance and solace from their religion in coping with the issues of these normal life stages. Just about every religion has some form of ritual for baby blessings, comings of age, weddings, and funerals. These life passages are like the major geographical features that appear on all maps.

As Paganism matures into a fully functioning religion, I think caring and responsible elders should be thinking about how we might best serve these normal needs. Simply put: people of different ages and different levels of spiritual involvement need different kinds of spiritual support, challenge, and guidance from their faith communities. All of their different needs are legitimate.

Now, look back at Erikson's model depicting the stages. Notice that each of the crises is portrayed as binary. One choice is considered good and the other bad. This either/or thinking is rooted in a monotheistic worldview. Where there is only one God, one single central point of reference for goodness, any given choice must be either more or less Godly. (Some fanatics even reject the idea of shadings; for them every choice is either Godly or ungodly. They might judge a harmless delight like music to be sinful, because it distracts from prayer.)

Here is another important example of how very basic theological orientation shapes our understandings of real-life situations. Even for most Pagans, the cultural habit of dualism is so deeply instilled that it seems instinctive or intuitive. Our change of faith hasn't yet reached that far down. But it could.

Different does not have to mean better or worse for us. As polytheists, we can conceive of many different ways to be Godly, in accord with our many different God/desses. But how do we get from deeply ingrained habits of dualistic thought to a more open, polycentric, "both/and" understanding of the world? By magic, of course.

Magic is the art of changing consciousness in accordance with will. One important magical technique is the power of naming. The language we use deeply influences the way we think. (This principle is also known to secular scholars, who call it the *Sapir-Whorf hypothesis*.) Consider what happens when we give other names to the attitudes Erikson judges to be unhealthy, names that mean the same thing but imply approval rather than disapproval:

- confusion becomes adaptability
- isolation becomes autonomy
- self-absorption becomes prudence
- despair becomes realism

These other, equally good attitudes can balance and complement those that Erikson deemed good instead of negating them. Both/and thinking gives us a much wider range of good choices. It also demands more thought, more care, and more responsibility to make the choices that are most appropriate for our own needs and goals. What's best for me may not be best for you.

In Pagan jargon, each pair of alternative responses in Erikson's model is a *polarity*. A polarity is something like a spectrum: both ends are good, but reciprocal. Coming closer to one inevitably takes you further from the other. More of either response surely means less of the other. Yet each can be taken to a damaging extreme unless it is balanced by the other. Balance is the key.

Remember, though, that there are two ways to stay in balance: neither/nor or both/and. Both are even-handed. Either can be appropriate, depending on circumstances. Some restrictions are real, others are falsely imposed by culture or habit. The wise will know the difference. An it harm none, do what you will!

So, Erikson identified four post-puberty life stages, and wrote that each one brings us to a developmental cusp and requires a particular decision. What would it look like if each of those four decisions were framed in terms of polarity instead of dualism? Like this:

Polarity-based Revision of Erikson's Model

AGE	DANGER OF IMBALANCE	AFFILIATION	BALANCE ("VIRTUE")	AUTONOMY	DANGER OF IMBALANCE
Adolescence	fanaticism, rigidity	cohesive identity	values, ideals (FIDELITY)	adaptability, flexibility	anomie, aimlessness
Early Adulthood	promiscuity	intimacy	family and community (LOVE)	autonomy	isolation
Mature Adulthood	over-extension, burnout	generosity	generativity (CARE)	assertive-ness, prudence	selfishness, hoarding
Elder	despair	realism, acceptance	serenity (WISDOM)	courage, integrity	denial

For me, this revised model is a far more accurate and useful depiction of adult development, without reference to religion. It's also a lot more consonant with Pagan understandings of the world. Tarot readers can probably relate this chart to cards that image balance, like the Chariot or the High Priestess. Ceremonialists and others who work with Cabala might compare this model with the symbol of the Middle Pillar that stands between Mercy and Severity. Greek reconstructionists can recognize the ancient ideal of the Golden Mean. Analogies exist across the wide range of holistic systems.

Even as adapted, the model is still not perfect. I suspect no abstract system can ever perfectly represent all the complexity of any living reality.

First, notice that Erikson's model is all about the relationship between self and others. My revision is directed towards finding the middle way between unhealthy enmeshment and equally unhealthy isolation. But relationships are not our only adult concern. Freud identified two: love and work. In addition to our very real need for affiliation, intimacy, and community, we have a parallel need for meaningful work and the sense of empowerment and self-esteem that it brings us. Most of us also need to earn a living, but even the few who are independently wealthy need to do something creative and useful in this world for their own satisfaction.

For our purposes as spiritual mentors, there is another human need: conscious contact with the Ancient Gods. It seems that this additional need is most likely to make itself known after the first two needs are reasonably fulfilled. In any case, a healthy and stable personality makes a far better channel for the awen.

Second, not all of these stages are inevitable and irreversible. Birth, growth, puberty, menopause or andropause, and death happen to all of us, and cannot be undone. But we don't all marry, and some of us divorce. Some marriages are childless. Some careers unwind, either because of external circumstances like technological or economic change, or because of mental or physical illness. Some people change careers successfully once or more during their adulthood.

Love and work, the things that matter most of all to us, don't just come without effort. They can be lost through neglect or through active bad choices. It seems that, within our culture, life has become more complex and more fluid since Erikson's time. Erikson's theory doesn't tell us anything at all about the ebbs and flows of contemporary adult life. For that, we need to use a different model.

Various models of human development might be regarded as overlays. Each researcher or theorist noticed some details but missed others. In theory, if we use the same scale, we could sketch each one on a transparency, then superimpose them. The result would have all the details combined, forming a more complete picture, but one perhaps too complicated for us to read. That's why we abstract in the first place.

Instead of overlays, think about binocular vision, a combination of perspectives instead of a simple increase of detail. Each of our two eyes views objects from a slightly different angle. By holding two perspectives simultaneously, we can see in depth. Similarly, working with more than one model of human growth (or any other reality, including the Sacred) allows us to understand it more deeply.

So let's consider a different secular model.

MASLOW'S NEEDS

Abraham Maslow (1908–1970), a contemporary of Erik Erikson's, became a psychologist during a period when two schools of thought — behaviorism and psychoanalysis — competed for ascendancy. Neither satisfied him, so he struck out on his own path. His new ideas became the basis of a third school, called humanistic psychology. Most of the exciting and interesting trends in contemporary psychological thought can trace at least part of their roots back to Maslow.[3]

One of Maslow's many important contributions was his concept that human needs are what he called *hierarchical*. We'd be more comfortable with the term *sequential*. Either way, the point is that the most basic need (or need cluster) must be satisfied before we even notice the next one, and so on through these five steps:

1. Survival needs: air, water, food, sleep, shelter for today.
2. Security needs: reason to expect that survival needs will be met for the foreseeable future.
3. Affiliative needs: a sense of connection, family, friends (love).
4. Self-esteem needs: respect, a sense of worthiness (meaningful work).

5. Self-actualization needs: deep satisfaction, the belief that one has fulfilled one's innate potential and lived well.

Here are some insights that Maslow's model can add to Erikson's:

- Work is as important as love and each is presented as an independent step.
- The steps are not age graded. In this understanding, people approach each step when they have worked through the one before. There's no implication of "ready or not." Instead of carrying deficiencies through all subsequent stages, you simply stay where you are until you are ready to proceed. The person who does not move through these steps may be considered stagnant or a victim of circumstances, but not sick.

  On the other hand, Erikson's model reminds us that people usually do approach particular growth points at particular ages. Bodily changes and changes in cultural expectations strongly influence people, even if they do not force anything on them. Getting out of synch with what is normal for one's age can induce both psychological and social problems.
- The sad reality is that people can travel both ways on this staircase. People get sick or injured, lose their jobs, divorce. Whole populations regress to security needs if fanatics seize control of their country. If physical or material or emotional security dissolves, a person may become completely preoccupied with rebuilding their base, and temporarily lack spare energy for creative self-expression or spiritual development.

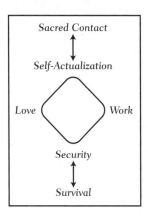

Sacred Contact

Self-Actualization

Love   Work

Security

Survival

REVISION OF MASLOW'S
HEIRARCHY OF NEEDS

Each model is incomplete. Each augments the other. Each, in my opinion, can be improved. The diagram at the left shows two small changes I made to Maslow's model. Some things to notice about it:

• In my observation, love and work are not sequential, but simultaneous. Establishing a career is just as important as finding a mate. Together, these two age-related tasks form an *and-gate*, a gate that requires both of two keys. The keys are about finding focus and making commitments in the two major areas, settling in after the exploratory period of adolescence. Erikson's early adulthood stage is typically devoted to passing through this gate, which leads into sound maturity.

• Self-actualization is Maslow's term for fullness of life. This is related to, but more inclusive than, Erikson's notion of generativity. It's possible to fulfill personal potentials and touch the future without any direct service to the young — by creating a legacy of scholarship or art, for example. Not every Pagan elder has to become a group leader or mentor.

• I've added an extra step: Sacred Contact. Secular counselors can work just as well as we can — and maybe better — with all the ordinary issues of adulthood. As spiritual mentors, our special task is assisting people to develop Sacred Contact.

Remember, though, that the way people work through all the prior steps makes a big difference in how well they can approach this one. Also, if any of your students experience losses that require them to focus their attention and energy on one of the "lower" steps, you will surely want to offer comfort and whatever guidance you can. Maslow shows us *why* spiritual mentors should become familiar with the full range of adult development and its potential problems.

Maslow's understandings are both more flexible and more inclusive than Erikson's. Erikson provides a structural frame connecting Maslow's steps to chronological age. Each corrects and completes the other. Although both models are secular, spiritual mentors of all religions need to understand them, for secular issues of adult development concern people of all religions or none.

A person can live well without ever pursuing inner spiritual growth. Love, work, and self-actualization are preliminary to mysticism — the proper preparations. Skipping over these priorities can lead to some very peculiar interpretations of "holiness."

Pagan mentors, elders, and teachers of Earth religion certainly should never separate *Godly* from *worldly* as some others do. Our core theological orientation, panentheism, directs us to learn all we can about everyday human concerns because all of life is included in the Sacred. Our public rituals, along with all exoteric aspects of our religion, should help us live daily life well, in proud accordance with Pagan values. Daily life then becomes a strong foundation for esoteric exploration and Sacred Contact.

All that being said, this book is about nurturing advanced Pagan spiritual development. If this chapter is laying out an outline map, spiritual exploration is not yet on it. Even though I added Sacred Contact to Maslow's model, I've simply pointed to the end of one particular page of a road atlas. There's nothing in either Erikson's or Maslow's model that gives us any notion of how people choose or travel a religious path. You might say they stop just before our major role as mentors begins. We need a model that goes beyond secular self-actualization.

Before anybody can sanely explore the advanced mysticism associated with any religion, they have to be or become a well-informed and active lay practitioner. This could mean devoutly following the religion of your birth. But that's not the story for most of us — not yet.

I'm a convert, and probably so are you. Very few of us were raised as Pagans. Most of us come to this religion in adulthood, by conscious choice. Some Pagan elders find satisfaction in welcoming newcomers to our community, helping them to find their way around. It's good for all of us to reflect upon the process of change that most of us have experienced.

Among ourselves, we don't call new Pagan affiliation *conversion* at all; we call it *homecoming*. The difference is not trivial. Remember, language shapes thought. Most religions expect conversion to be a transformative experience. They expect new adherents to think, behave, and even speak differently, utterly renouncing their old ways. In contrast, we say that "you don't become a Pagan; you find out that there's a name for what you already were, and a community of others who feel the same way."

All we really expect from a new homecomer is a deep sigh of relief. Certainly we have our community mores and customs. We'll explore them in Chapter 6. However, instead of indoctrinating or resocializing newcomers, we like to believe that they come to us because they find us already feeling and doing the very things that made them misfits in their previous faith communities. They find the home they never thought existed for them. That's what it felt like for me. How about you?

It's not that simple, of course. Whoever comes home as an adult has left a previous home. Although it was less satisfactory, still there are aspects they'll miss and baggage they'll carry along. And anybody who has ever moved house — even to a much better location — knows how disorienting and how much work it can be.

At this critical part of the path the scale changes, allowing the map to show more detail. Here's a staged model that specifically describes the process of religious conversion.

RAMBO'S STAGES OF CONVERSION

Lewis R. Rambo is Professor of Psychology and Religion at the San Francisco Theological Seminary. His well-respected book *Understanding Religious Conversion*[4] presents this comprehensive seven-step model of the conversion process.

1. Context

This is the starting point, made up of everything that has brought the person to where they are now: their upbringing, their educational background, their work, their social network, the cultural trends around them. Their previous religious training and experience. Their mental health and social skills. Their core values.

The Erikson and Maslow models can be of great help in understanding a seeker's life context: all the intellectual, emotional, and spiritual resources available to them at any moment in their lives, including the crisis point. In turbulent moments of conversion or in periods of gradual growth, seekers can only start from where they are. Mentors will be more helpful if they understand the seeker's general direction and present location.

The risk of this phase — I think it's premature to call it a challenge — is conventionality or stagnation. People may follow the forms of their birth tradition by rote, never really probing their deeper meanings or striving for congruent lives. Absent social pressure to attend services, they may completely ignore the religious aspects of life. As a religiously committed person, I believe atheism is far more honest than robotic conventional practice.

2. Crisis

This second phase is nothing but challenge. Something happens to destabilize a person's religious identity.

It might be a sudden and painful discovery. Adolescents who are already struggling to find their personal values and identity are particularly vulnerable to disillusionment. Their trust may be shattered when they learn that religious tales they were told as children are not factual. The world was not assembled in six days, and neither did the magician Gwydion make a maiden out of flowers to be his young nephew's bride. Worse, they may find that a respected religious leader has behaved inappropriately. Contradictions of this sort may become intolerable, forcing the seeker to leave where they are, even if they have nowhere else to go.

At any age, traumatic shock — serious injury or illness, bereavement, etc. — can induce a religious crisis. So can spiritual emergency — an unexpected and overwhelming mystical experience that challenges settled beliefs or social roles. In fact, traumatic shock can precipitate a spiritual emergency. Spiritual emergency may look just like psychosis, but it's really more like psycho-spiritual growing pains (more details in Chapter 5).

Simple dissatisfaction, a hunger for more, can set off a quieter kind of religious crisis, more typical of a mature person who has reached the top of Maslow's secular hierarchy. Often a religious crisis can be understood or reframed as a Sacred call.

The real challenge of any crisis is to find a way to use it as an opportunity for growth. Pagans can receive growth-provoking crisis as the gift of the Crone, of "She who breaks the dams when the waters have become stagnant."

3. Quest

The person in crisis searches for helpful alternative approaches, within or beyond their original faith tradition. There are many ways to gather information: reading, broadcast media, visits to houses of worship, talking with friends of different religions.

People in the quest stage may show up at open rituals and approach elders afterwards with copious questions. Elders who respond well to this sort of curiosity may find themselves acting as resource people to new seekers. Since my coven maintains a Web site for adult seekers,[5] I occasionally receive emails from people on quest.

If you meet a seeker who is on quest because of disillusion or profound disagreement with their birth tradition, first try to help them explore the progressive alternatives within that original community. Most mainstream religions contain internal minorities and advocacy groups that are feminist, environmentally oriented, supportive of gay rights, etc. Perhaps such groups will meet their need, and spare them the unpleasant side effects of a change of religion. Nobody should leave their original faith unless they really have to. Furthermore, the Pagan community only wants those who are coming home to us from joyful choice.

Please notice that seekers on a quest are still looking at spiritual resources outside of themselves. This is not inner exploration yet, but the necessary precursor, the search for a theological model that offers an entry point and a faith community that provides a secure base camp.

The challenge of the quest stage is to reach the bridge that crosses from anger to hope. Even if the trauma that drove them from their previous affiliation was directly caused by clergy corruption, oppressive theological models, etc., running away will only get them . . . away. They need to actually get somewhere else, and hopefully somewhere better. Healthy reaffiliation requires that we go towards something good, not just away from something bad.

4. Encounter

The seeker meets somebody, or notices that someone they already know is devout and active in the practice of their religion. If they perceive this person as truly spiritual — honest, kind, wise, and grounded — they may choose to explore the same path. The friend whose spirituality attracted the seeker may answer their questions, loan them reading material, take them along to services, or even introduce them to a clergy member who can provide more information.

Some faith groups actively proselytize. They send out missionaries. But even in nonproselytizing communities like ours, personal contact is a normal step in the process of conversion. The way we live our faith is the beacon that quietly guides our own back home.

5. Interaction

The seeker finds a religious community that seems to suit them better. They spend some period as a guest or a participant observer, perhaps attending public rituals, learning the customs, getting to know the people. Some faith communities offer structured introductory classes for adults who are considering conversion.

The challenge of this phase is discernment. Interaction, as Rambo defines it, is like courtship: there's a halo effect. People are welcoming and supportive to newcomers. Internal problems are backstage where seekers are unlikely to see them. Seekers need clear perception and critical thinking skills to penetrate the glow, to check whether this group's theology, ritual practice, etc. are consonant with the seeker's core values, the promptings of their inner guides. Those who commit in haste recant at leisure, usually loudly and bitterly, sometimes at the local courthouse.

6. Commitment

The seeker formally, usually ritually, joins the new faith community. By doing so, they take on all the ritual and moral obligations of membership. In some local areas, Pagans are now developing long-needed rituals to mark and celebrate the moment when a person joins our laity — their homecoming.

For Pagans, the challenge of the commitment stage is "coming out," informing non-Pagan family and friends. Many of them are still ignorant about our religion. Hostile stereotypes abound, and sometimes lead to cruel discrimination. Telling people about an attraction to or affiliation with Paganism can expose us to considerable risk. Our people have traditions of secrecy, believed to go back to Inquisitorial times when the risk was far more dire than job loss.

Certainly we are under no religious mandate to "bear witness" to our faith. But we have learned from the gay experience that secrecy is inimical to an authentic life, and detrimental to mental health. Elders, particularly those who have negotiated their own coming out with relatively little damage, may want to help newcomers work through this difficult set of choices.

7. Outcomes[6]

The person participates fully in the new faith community, while continuing to learn more about its ways. Their hopes may be fulfilled or disappointed. Some people cycle through this model several times before they find a religion that truly meets their needs.

There may be repercussions from people who disapprove of the conversion, particularly family members or former friends. If the new religion is socially unpopular, a so-called "cult," the new member may face difficulties with employment, housing, or even child custody. Not long ago, converts to unfamiliar or unpopular religions also risked legalized kidnapping and coercive pressure towards deconversion.

It's also entirely possible that the seeker will find all that was sought: Sacred Contact, a symbol system consonant with their core values, a ritual system that nurtures their inner life, a congruent ethical code, and a supportive community. So mote it be!

Working with Rambo's Stages of Conversion

Rambo proposes that all conversion processes begin with some sort of crisis. I agree, especially if crisis is broadly defined to mean any destabilizing experience, from spiritual break-through to traumatic shock. But people need very different kinds of help in working through these very different types of crisis. Here are just a few of the stories Pagan mentors may hear from new homecomers:

- A fifteen-year-old, in the midst of adolescent identity crisis, is sexually molested by a clergy member.
- A parent, previously comfortable in their marriage, career, and religious affiliation, discovers that their teenage child has been sexually molested by a clergy member.
- A college student reads a book that challenges the religious teachings they received in a happy childhood. The evidence and logic in the book are strongly persuasive.

- A midlife professional, with no previous interest in religion, takes up meditation for stress relief and has a surprising experience of Sacred Contact. They have no idea what this means or what they should do about it. They may even be worried about losing their grip on reality.
- A teenager discovers an apparent contradiction within the teachings of their religion, or a conflict between religious teachings and their own experiences and values. When they raise the question with a clergy member, the clergy member becomes angry and tells the youngster that it is improper to question received wisdom.
- A college student has always believed what their religious tradition taught about justice and stewardship. Now they discover that the endowment funds that support the institutional structure of their religion are invested in third-world prison factories or domestic strip mines.
- A young married couple who have not previously questioned their conventional religious upbringing lose their cherished baby to Sudden Infant Death Syndrome. At the funeral, the officiating clergy member tells them not to question the will of Deity.

CASE STUDIES

All of the situations listed above can be used in elders' workshops or support groups. They can serve as role-plays, as the bases for brainstorm or mind-map exercises, or simply as starting points for group discussions. Even better, you can evoke situations directly from the group — people learn a lot from hearing others' perceptions and suggestions about the situations they are actually working with.

One way to let people present situations for group exploration without risk of embarrassment is to place some blank note cards, pens, and a basket in an unobtrusive spot in the workshop room. (For a bit of humor, clean up an old coffee can and label it "WORMS".) Explain at the beginning of the workshop that participants can write about their own perplexing situations on these cards, anonymously if they wish, and add them to the basket or the can of worms. Then cards can be pulled at random. Or, if there is a facilitator, the facilitator can review the cards during a break and choose which ones to present. (For more about learning methods, see Chapter 7.)

As a Pagan mentor, you'll probably be meeting people in the interaction stage, while they are participating in public Pagan rituals and activities and deciding whether they want to commit to our lifeways. They may ask you for some guidance or assistance. To do this well, it helps to understand — quite literally — where they are coming from. Using all three models — Erikson's, Maslow's, and Rambo's — can help you do this in depth and in detail. Here are the central concerns:

1. What was the nature and intensity of their religious crisis?
2. What was their background developmental level when the crisis hit? Which life issues were focal for them at that time?

If their crisis was a frightening spiritual emergency, they'll need to learn more about navigating altered states of consciousness. If the seeker is a young person engaged in their normal adolescent identity crisis, you can expect a longer, more turbulent quest than if they were already settled in the more basic areas of marriage and career. On the other hand, if they believed they were comfortably settled and it all fell apart for them in trauma, they will need to work through a mourning process before they are truly free to move on. The possible permutations are endless.

Remember to listen, to let the seeker set the agenda, to act as a resource person rather than a judge. They are not seeking esoteric inner exploration right now. That may come later or never. For now, they are wondering whether our ways can help them stabilize and recover from their current crisis. They are simply considering whether to become a lay Pagan. The only question on the table is how we can best help them, not how to take advantage of their distress by proselytizing them.

When approaching or working through a life transition, it's good to look back, to understand and appreciate the path we've walked so far. Here's an exercise that I've found particularly useful. Please do it yourself before you suggest it to a seeker or student (that goes for every other exercise in this book!).

TIMELINE EXERCISE

You'll need some legal-sized paper, or you can tape two sheets of letter-sized paper together to make a longer sheet. Also have some colored pens or crayons handy. Hold the paper in the "landscape" orientation, so the long part is horizontal rather than vertical. Date the paper and draw a plain black line all the way across it, horizontally, about halfway from top to bottom.

Take a few minutes to ground and center yourself, and to reflect on those significant events and people in your life, on all that has brought you to the present moment. Then, in color, draw a line that represents your ups and downs. Some will be higher or lower than others. Some will be more closely spaced, others farther apart. Finally, label them. If you like, you can draw symbols or pictures that relate to what was going on. One artistically trained student of mine drew no pictures at all. He covered the page with writing, using different ink colors, lettering styles, and sizes to create a striking abstract design of his life.

Put it away for a couple of days, then look at it again. See if you can identify moments of crisis, periods of intense exploration, significant encounters with people, other experience that were, for you, epiphanies. Feel free to add words, symbols, or pictures to the design. Save it.

It's a good idea to repeat this exercise once a year, or at times of particularly intense change. Do not look at any of the old ones for at least a week before you draw a new timeline. Make the comparisons, if at all, when you're reviewing the latest one, to better understand your progress.

If you're keeping a journal, write about what you learned from this exercise. If you're not, start one. (For more about journals, see Chapter 5.)

Eventually, the person may choose to become part of the Pagan community. This passage is significant, actually life changing, even though it too often goes unmarked. If the interaction phase is something like a courtship, commitment is much like a marriage. We do this joyfully, but not casually. As someone reaches the decision point, they need to know the callings of their own heart. These questions in the following exercise may help. (Again, work through the exercise yourself before assigning it to a student.)

QUESTIONS FOR PEOPLE CONSIDERING COMMITMENT
- What do you experience as Sacred in your life?
- What is your source of hope? of pride? of power?
- To what are you loyal? To what are you devoted?
- For what are you thankful?

- Where do you find nurturance?
- Which Deity guides or empowers you?
- How would that Deity describe you?
- Whom or what do you trust? Whom or what do you fear?
- What are you most inspiring goals, your most Sacred hopes?
- With whom do you share these things? What are your sources of human guidance or support? Whom do you trust?

Ponder these questions. Write your answers in your journal privately. If you like, you can discuss them with significant others, including your mentor.

If you are in an intimate, bonded relationship, I strongly suggest that you discuss your answers with your lifemate. You should be discussing all aspects of your potential change of religion with your mate, who will inevitably be deeply affected by your decision.

After meditating and dreaming on the answers for a few days, see if they change at all. Then ask yourself similar questions about the group you are considering joining. See how well your answers fit together.

We have no guarantee that this will be our path forever. There may be more crises and more changes yet to come. We certainly shouldn't swear to what we can't know for sure. Still, any such commitment should be based on hope, desire, and a reasonable prediction that this religious affiliation will last through life. Just like marriage.

Another and even more important similarity to marriage is that commitment is a gateway, not a dead end. Living and learning do not end with that ritual. If it stagnates, it dies. There's no such thing as "happily ever after," only more growth in love, understanding, and faith.

Faith. Most people hearing the word *faith* understand it as "belief in the absence of evidence or logic." Even most dictionaries have similar definitions. But that definition leads nowhere good. Setting faith in opposition to critical thinking makes us vulnerable to every opportunistic ideologue, religious or political. This is the "faith" of fundamentalists. Modern theology has an entirely different understanding of the word.

Faith, for our purposes, is not a matter of taking some improbable or unprovable tale as fact, nor assenting to any kind of untestable assertion about the unknowable. It is not anybody's opiate, not a collection of glib explanations for life's tragedies. It should not mute our awareness of mystery; rather, it should allow us to live well even though we have incomplete knowledge. It is most certainly not a matter of replacing evidence and logic with appeals to any form of authority.

Instead, faith is right relationship with the Entheoi and with one another. Our understanding of this relationship is preverbal, so basic and intrinsic to our being that we are often not consciously aware of it at all, but still it guides us through life. We experience faith as a "meaning system," a central organizing paradigm, and we express faith through myth and metaphor, and through behavior. To have faith in this sense is to choose to live on the assumption that our relationship with the Entheoi is composed of love and trust. Faith is not what we believe or say, but how we act. Faith shines through a congruent life.[7]

Religion can be understood as a process by which a community strives, through a series of successive approximations, to manifest faith and to nurture faith in one another. Therefore we work, individually and together, to clarify our understanding, to refine our symbolic expression, and to live our lives in accordance with our faith.

And this brings us to the last, and most directly relevant, of the non-Pagan staged models of adult development in this chapter.

FOWLER'S STAGES OF FAITH

James W. Fowler is Director of the Center for Ethics at Emory University. His book, *Stages of Faith*,[8] first published in 1981, has been through multiple printings and many translations and is still in print. Fowler's ideas have had a very strong and widespread influence on our understanding of how people mature in religious faith.

Fowler drew on his own experience with religious formation, gained by working at a retreat center and on the stage theory of Erik Erikson, which I discussed earlier in this chapter. Another of his sources was Lawrence Kohlberg, whose ideas about moral development will appear in Chapter 6. Jean Piaget was also important to Fowler's analysis, but Piaget's work on cognitive development in young children is outside the scope of this book.

Erikson, Kohlberg, and Piaget all created sequential, staged models of development. Fowler's model synthesizes them and applies their insights to the area of faith development. Here's an overview of Fowler's model:

Fowler's Stages of Faith

STAGE	TYPICAL AGE RANGE
1. Intuitive-Projective faith	3–6
2. Mythic-Literal faith	6–12
3. Synthetic-Conventional faith	13+

4. Individuative-Reflective faith	21+
5. Conjunctive faith	35+
6. Universalizing faith	60+

General Comments about Fowler's Model

Fowler's model was derived from a great deal of field research. Fowler and his associates interviewed over three hundred Christians and Jews in the United States and Canada, trying for a proper balance of age and gender. Their results were later replicated by others in India, Liberia, and Malaysia, based on interviews with Hindus and Muslims as well as more Christians. The questions that were included in the structured interviews and a full statistical breakdown of responses are included as appendices in *Stages of Faith*.

The stage descriptions were developed by identifying common themes in the interview responses. The book includes a chapter on each stage, with extensive quotations from the interview transcripts for all but the last stage. Obviously, they could not conduct in-depth interviews with babies, so Fowler's stages begin with age three. I won't be discussing Stages 1 and 2, which cover the childhood years. Our central concern, as mentors of adults, is with Fowler's Stages 3–5.

Stage 6 was mostly based on assumptions about some admired (and admirable) public figures, constructed from accounts in the public media rather than from direct interviews. Out of all those who were interviewed, only one elderly man was rated at Stage 6. Accordingly, I consider Stage 6 to be an ideal type rather than a realistic category. Ideal types serve as important models for living well.

Historical or public figures can be known only distantly. We have no knowledge of their inner motivations or the messy details of their close relationships. We can idealize them, taking their stories as "navigational stars" by which we can steer. We can adopt them as our intellectual or spiritual ancestors, our personal or collective Mighty Dead. (More about the Mighty Dead in Chapter 7.)

Please notice that for Stages 3–6, only a starting age is shown. After Stage 3, these are really only *potential* starting ages. In Fowler's model, like Maslow's, progress is not inevitable. In fact, most lay people — and many clergy — of any religion stay at Stage 3 or 4 for their whole lives.

This is a problem for any community of faith, even large congregations. It's a worse problem for our small groups, where peer pressure can be stronger. Groups of any size tend to establish a *modal developmental level*, which Fowler defines as "the average expectable level of development for adults in a given community." Most groups nurture and support their members' growth up to that modal level, then ignore or even punish further development.[9] Those who go beyond the group's modal level, or who question received wisdom, seem like heretics to conventional believers. The developmental level attained by a group leader, or individual spiritual mentor, also tends to impose a ceiling on the development of members or students.

I'd like to take a closer look now at the three realistic stages of adult faith development. Most of our students will fit into one of these.

Stage 3: Synthetic-Conventional Faith

Stage 3 normally emerges during adolescence. Teenagers need to learn who they are apart from their parents, but are not yet ready for full independence. As a step towards it, they may follow fads, associate themselves with subcultures, adopt ideologies. All those ironic jokes about the stringent conformity of teen "nonconformists" are based on real observation.

In Stage 3, people may give their loyalty to a group, a creed, or a cause outside themselves. They interpret religious metaphors literally, regarding them as either facts or lies. They rely on external authority, either in formal positions or roles (as long as the person occupying the role appears to be worthy) or perhaps in a group or organization as a whole. Their ethics are based on a need to avoid feeling ashamed before others and a desire for external approval. They are conformists, people-pleasers.

Teens may seem fickle or faddish as they cycle through a series of passionate affiliations, or they may stay with the same rigid ideology — and in Stage 3 — for the rest of their lives.

Rambo, whose book was published more than ten years after Fowler's, could not have influenced Fowler, but I think their ideas are synergetic.

By combining their perspectives, I would speculate that a teen who "tries on" a variety of ideologies or religious practices as part of a normal Eriksonian identity quest may, in young adulthood, settle in to their birth tradition or might, with care and thought, choose to join another faith group. As they mature, they may feel called to pursue intense spiritual development. Or they may discover that they just are not religiously inclined, and go on to make satisfying lives without much religious participation. They'll find the type and level of religious involvement that best serves their own needs.

But the adolescent seeker who is thrown into a religious crisis by trauma or disillusion before they are stable in their own identity is much more like a refugee than an explorer. Their quest is for psycho-spiritual safety and security much more than it is for self-definition or self-actualization. They may actually feel safer in a group that enforces dogma and requires obedience than they would with the freedom and personal responsibility found among more liberal religious groups. If they find a group that is authoritarian but honest, fair, and kindly, they may stay right there forever, becoming a "true believer."[10] The modal developmental level of authoritarian groups is likely to be conventional, which adds to the probability of such arrested development. If they settle into an authoritarian group that later turns out to be corrupt, they'll be much more hurt, of course, than they were in the first crisis. That's the bad risk.

Religious crisis can be induced by theological contradictions or personal misconduct of leaders in the teen's birth tradition. All we can do about that is offer them a nonauthoritarian environment, an option for their healing, knowing that only those who were already strong enough to flourish in freedom will be able to heal among us. Nor should we ever use their vulnerability to try to recruit them to our ways. Anyone who comes home to us should come by their own free and happy choice.

We may only rarely be able to help, but we can make very sure we do no harm to the young. Remember that any overwhelming spiritual experience can be traumatic and unsustainable for the unprepared. An overly zealous spiritual mentor, with good intentions but poor judgment, might teach advanced techniques such as trance practices prematurely. If frightening visions result, unformed young personalities could go into spiritual emergency. Panic and backlash could send the youngster straight to the nearest authoritarian group or leader. The result: another true believer, saved from their pagan ways, on the anticult speaker circuit. In short: arrested development for the adolescent; more public misinformation for us to deal with.

I only wish that were the worst that could happen. History teaches otherwise. Remember, you've read about this: young girls scrying in egg whites, trying to glimpse their future husbands; visions, sudden and terrifyingly intense; youth in panic; adults using the panic for their own political ends; twenty people unjustly slain in Salem, MA in 1692. Let's not go that way again.

Stage 4: Individuative-Reflective Faith

The potential for transition to Stage 4 appears as the person moves into their early twenties and assumes full responsibility for their own life. Perhaps they left their parents' home some years earlier. Most, however, went to college or entered military service. They were still living under institutional conditions, relieved (or deprived, if you prefer) of many choices and responsibilities. Now, at least outside of working hours, their lives will be their own to manage. During these years, they will choose an occupation and probably also a mate. They will begin working towards long-range goals.

All of that is secular. For some people, these secular changes evoke very parallel changes in religious orientation. Mostly this is not a change of affiliation but an assumption of responsibility. From now on, their perceptions of the Sacred will not be determined for them by text or teacher. Instead, they will weigh the scriptures they read and the teachings they hear against their own experiences and values. They will form their own conclusions, create their own synthesis, adapt their practice to their own understandings and needs. They will find their own authority within themselves. What they actually do may be identical to the behavior of a conventional co-religionist, but they will choose on a very different basis: autonomy rather than habit or obedience.

They interpret religious metaphors in terms of meaning rather than literal fact, but often shallowly, as simple signs. Their ethics are based on personal pride and a healthy desire for self-esteem. They want to know, inside themselves, that they are doing the right thing. They make decisions based on self-determined but abstract principles of right and wrong, fairness, and justice.

Children are taught religion in a childish way, through simple stories and rules. People at Stage 3, wanting to be different but not quite ready to grow up, may substitute some other set of stories and rules. Some never discover the depth and complexity of mature religion. For them, being religious still means believing and behaving as you are told, even when it makes no sense at all. As they move into autonomous early adulthood, if that's all they think religion is, they will probably reject it completely. The potential for growing into individuative faith is diverted into an arid sort of freedom, at least for some period of time.

Others moving into adulthood will give all their attention and energy to the age-related secular issues of building a marriage and a career. They don't overtly reject spirituality, but they do defer it, maybe forever. They will probably maintain some loose connection with their family's religion, attending services for major holidays and life passages. I suspect that if somebody like that is thrown into a religious crisis by severe disillusion or trauma, they are more likely to move aside into angry rejection than to regress to an authoritarian group.

Young adults who are religiously oriented, although their primary focus is on developing adult lifestyles at this stage, will want to make life choices that are in accord with religious values and principles. If confronted with problems or major decisions, they may seek the advice of an elder. Strictly speaking, assistance of this sort is more like pastoral counseling than spiritual mentoring. Still, if you are asked for this kind of help, much of the information in Chapter 3 is equally applicable.

There's one special case: future clergy in many religions attend seminary in their early twenties while their age mates train for other professions. Similarly, most members of my coven's preinitiatory study group are recent college graduates. For this group, religion is a career choice, although the work will be part-time and unpaid. Many of the Pagan Traditions forbid or discourage accepting payment for religious work.

Our priest/esses are like musicians and poets: they know they will also need to find a trade or profession that will provide a livelihood while they do their religious work. Mentors teach this mostly by example, by maintaining a visible balance between our secular careers, our family lives, and our religious vocations. The best service you can give your students is to let your own struggle show.

The relationship between advanced spiritual work and clergy preparation is also complicated. People preparing for clergy roles generally begin exploring the inner paths earlier than others. They need to. The developmental level attained by a teacher or leader tends to set the modal developmental level for their future students or congregants. It's hard — maybe impossible — to guide people to places you haven't been; it's hard not to resent students who advance beyond their own teachers.

Personal spirituality can be nurtured in an individual mentoring relationship or in a group. Which will work better depends on the personalities concerned. But advanced spiritual development, however necessary, is not sufficient. Clergy need good interpersonal and administrative skills as well. These can only be learned in a group context.

So I think young adults who feel called to serve as Pagan clergy should be trained within groups: Wiccan covens, Druid groves, Asatru hofs, etc. Of course, many mentors are also group leaders. If you're not, or if this student works well with you personally but would not fit well into your group, I recommend you help them find a suitable group as soon as possible.

Nobody should rush through a stage. Living each faith stage — and each life stage — fully, doing its tasks and learning its lessons, is the best possible preparation for the next stage. To the normal developmental tasks of young adulthood, people in Faith Stage 4 add the dimension of exoteric religion, a source of nurturance and guidance.

For those who are religiously inclined, Stage 4 is the time to make a mature adult commitment to a particular religious tradition — probably the one in which they were raised. As self-directed, self-responsible adults, they can explore the meanings behind familiar stories they used to take literally. They can consider how ethical rules and ritual practices they once simply obeyed actually fit with their own experiences and values, then decide what behavior is right for them. As they build their lives around a mature religious core, they are also preparing themselves for later advanced exploration, becoming fit containers for the awen they may eventually seek and receive.

If we think of Pagan spiritual development as a path, at Stage 4 we assemble our gear.

Stage 5: Conjunctive Faith

The potential for Stage 5 opens up around the age of thirty. If the tasks of early adulthood have been well done, a person has a secure sense of personal identity and is settled in family and career.

Grandiose early dreams fade by midlife. Maybe we won't get rich or famous. Maybe we won't star on Broadway or be elected to the Senate. But we can have deep satisfaction and joy in our work, our families, and our faith. We can actualize our own potential, nurture the young, and influence the human future. We can come to terms with ourselves. This is middle age, the prime of life, the long, fruitful summer.

What secular psychologists call the "midlife crisis," astrologers have long recognized as the Saturn return. Here is how astrologer Maria Escudero describes it: "In a 30-year cycle, Saturn, the brutally fair 'lord of Karma,' cycles through each of the astrological houses, gifting each of us with the exact difficult lessons of responsibility, structure and limitation we most need, leading to mastery and adulthood at age 30."[11]

Rambo describes a gentle sort of religious crisis that happens when a person has achieved this integration and simply wants more.[12] More what? More quality. For the religiously inclined, more depth and intensity in their spiritual life.

People at the individuative-reflective stage open to their own deep minds and to the Otherworld that dwells at the Center of all. Being secure in their autonomy, they can balance and integrate their inner authority with the collective authority of cumulative tradition. Being secure in their religious affiliation, they can be open to learning the deep truth of other traditions as well, in true interfaith dialogue.

These are the ones who have gained a full belly of learning, can certainly think critically about the contents of their religion, and have also retrieved the ability to pray like a child. They have not regressed, but have gone forward, around the spiral, to a new synthesis of mind, heart, and spirit.

For them, religious metaphors are true symbols, complex and multivocal, linking humans to a Sacred reality that is ultimately beyond definition. They are able to suspend disbelief and judgment; to approach traditional lore and rituals in an openhearted, meditative manner; to be surprised, even changed, by their experience.

- They can live and function in an uncertain world, aware of the complexity and ambiguity around them. They are not looking for easy answers or quick fixes.
- They have chosen their religious affiliation with thought and care. They've made the Tradition their own through creative interaction with its lore and practices.

- Their thoughts and actions both manifest a deep and abiding concern for humankind and for Mother Earth.
- Their ethics are situational, based on true empathy and care.
- Their daily behavior is congruent with the values they profess.
- They have a realistic sense of their own strengths and weaknesses. They are working towards their own growth.
- They know and respect their own boundaries and equally respect the boundaries of others.

Stage 5 Pagans are ready to seek more consistent and conscious contact with the Entheoi. They are properly prepared to receive the awen and to use it for the good of all. Healthy advanced spiritual development for most people starts from this point.

STARTING POINT: SELF-ASSESSMENT

The exercise that follows is for both mentor and student, as are all the exercises in this book. Generally, you ought not ask a student to do anything you have not done yourself. More important, self-knowledge is a mentor's only real protection against damaging counter-transference. For the student, self-examination before undertaking intense inner exploration is comparable to getting a good physical exam before undertaking a serious exercise routine.

I borrowed and adapted the idea of taking a personal inventory from the Twelve-Step Programs. Like the Twelve Steps, our religious path is about personal growth. Although there's no core incompatibility between our practices and the Twelve Steps, there are significant differences of emphasis. These strongly influence the way in which we take inventory.

For us, the exercise is as much about gifts and strengths as it is about flaws or deficiencies. Most of all, it's about goals.

PERSONAL INVENTORY

All by yourself, in the privacy of your own heart and mind, take a searching and fearless look at your life as it is right now and as you would like it to be. Nobody's reading over your shoulder, so there's no need at all to deny or defend. Here are some possible starting questions. (No doubt many others will come up as you reflect on your own situation.)

- Are you the person you would like to be? Identify some things about yourself and your life that you like very much. Identify some others that you don't like at all. What about your life would you like to change, and in what direction? What do you mourn? At what do you rage? What do you celebrate? What do you miss? To what do you aspire?

- What would your life look like if you were to describe it in terms of a Tarot spread, the four elements, the seven planets, or whatever your favorite structure of understanding is? What myths do you think you may be living out right now? How are they guiding you well? How are they guiding you poorly?

- What contexts formed you (e.g., race, class, gender, culture, region, specific family history, specific personal history, etc.)? Which of these have given you pleasure and which are a source of distress or perhaps even trauma for you? Which of these still operate and which no longer apply? Did those that no longer apply form any ways of thinking or acting that no longer work for you, or discourage any that you perceive would be helpful to you now? As these contexts change, options open for personal change as well.

- Consider all areas of your life, not just the religious or spiritual aspects. How do you feel about your home situation, your love life, your friendships? Do you have any unfinished business with anyone of significance to you? What might you do to resolve it? What, if anything, would you like to change about your immediate environment, material or social? Are you adequately nurtured by yourself and by others?

- How do you feel about your career? Do you have adequate outlets — in or out of your day job — for self-expression? Do you feel like you are "somebody" in your immediate world, a contributing part of whatever communities you belong to? Where is the room for improvement?

- How do you feel about your physical and emotional health? What do you do for fun? Is there enough play and recreation in your life? Do you get enough rest and downtime? Do you want to make any changes in your life style?

- Have you any unfulfilled dreams, needs, or desires? How might you move towards fulfilling them? If you knew you had only a day to live, but with full comfort and mobility throughout it, how would you spend that day? that week? that month? that year? Which of those things could you reasonably be doing more of right now?

- To the extent that you can identify them, what are your obstacles? old hurts? unrealistic fears? outworn habits? joyless obligations? What can you do to clear the way for your own growth and fulfillment?

- What are your talents, gifts, strengths? Are you satisfied with how you have cultivated these up to now?

What are your next plans and goals? What are you curious about right now? What would you like to learn? How might you go about learning it?

- Do you feel secure in your contact with the Ancient Gods? Are you happy with your role in the Pagan community? What contributions would you like to make next? Is there something more you would like to receive from the community?

- What about yourself or your life do you hope will change? What can you do in the next week, month, year to move towards the changes you desire?

During this process, invite the participation of the Gods through divination, dream work, and meditation. You may also want to discuss the process with your mentor and your partner if you have one.

At this point, you have a great deal of information about yourself, and you probably need to make some sense of it. It's time to borrow another major piece of wisdom from the Twelve-Step Programs. Are you familiar with the *Serenity Prayer*? Here it is in Pagan adaptation:

> May the Ancient Gods help me to find within myself
> serenity to accept the things I cannot change,
> courage to change the things I can,
> and wisdom to know the difference.

Short prayers like this one work like affirmations. By frequent repetition, you install some habits of perceiving or reacting into your own deep mind. The *Serenity Prayer* is well worth using on that basis alone. It is also a very useful framework of analysis to use consciously in working with any problems or situations in your life, or with your life as a whole.

There probably are some things that you really want to change, but cannot: externally imposed conditions, physical limitations, poor choices made in your youth that are impossible to reverse, might-have-beens of all kinds. Don't suppress the feelings. Sorrow or anger might be entirely appropriate. But in the end, acceptance, however bitter, releases your energy to work on changing things where there is realistic hope of good results. Truth purifies.[13]

So, having filtered your self-assessment through the *Serenity Prayer*, you can now identify some realistic short- and midterm goals. These may be either remedial or developmental — both are part of the growth process. What are the steps that will take you from here to there? What resources will you need to gather to approach those steps? Just as you were willing to fully experience grief or anger, allow yourself to feel your hope and enthusiasm as they begin to build.

Now, as you have set some good goals, you might want to celebrate your renewed commitment through ritual. State your intentions within Sacred space. Ask your close friends to raise power to help you achieve your purpose. Perhaps consecrate some sort of talisman to hold this energy and act as a reminder.

As we grow, it's good to review our progress and set new goals based on more recent experience. So the personal inventory is not a one-time activity. You should take inventory as part of your preparation for any significant life passage. It's also a good idea to take inventory once a year. Between Samhain and Yule is traditionally a good time for taking inventory and generally for putting your house in order.

Growth comes in the dynamic interplay between action and reflection. Taking inventory is simply one technique for the reflection part of the process. This is a modern expression of a very ancient injunction: Know Thyself.

PAGAN PATHS

We have our own Pagan or magical models for growth. I've put more emphasis on the insights of non-Pagan researchers and theorists only because they are less likely to be familiar already to you. Now, reaching insights rooted in our own religion, we turn another page in the road atlas and discover another change of scale showing even more detail.

I find it interesting that many Pagan models are more cyclic than linear. Remember, for example, the Saturn return. The houses of the Zodiac each represent a particular aspect of human activity. As Saturn, symbolic of karma, cycles through each one, he presents us with appropriate challenges and lessons. Then he starts again, cycling through those same houses as long as we live, but each time in a deeper, stronger way. Each time we face a challenge, we have what we learned from all prior challenges as resources.

Maybe that tells us what is radically different about our Pagan, panentheistic path. We are not going somewhere away from normal life in search of the Gods. They are right here, right now. We were already with Them, in Them, and They in us, before we took the first step. The connection is already intact; all that changes is our awareness. It's not some exotic and arduous trek, it's an attentive walk around the block. The final and most detailed maps are of our own neighborhoods.[14]

1. Tarot

Neo-Paganism has roots deep in the Western Esoteric magical traditions. Tarot has been an important part of those traditions since at least the Renaissance. The Major Arcana cards are often interpreted as pictures of a staged developmental sequence known as *the Fool's Journey*.[15] Since I am not an expert on Tarot, I asked tarotist Elizabeth Genco for a brief introduction to the sequence. Here's what she wrote:

- *The Fool (Key 0).* As zero stands alone in the numerical sequence, the Fool stands alone, separate from the rest of the Major Arcana. The Fool is each of us as we travel through each stage. He is like a newborn at the beginning of the journey, naïve and filled with optimism. He will come to each stage with this same attitude of wonder: no judgments, no preconceived notions. He will grow and develop as he passes through the stages to emerge complete and whole at Key 21, The World. The Fool represents each of us on our own journey towards wholeness.

- *The Magician (Key 1).* The Magician represents the active principle. As we go through this stage, we learn how to concentrate and direct our will. We learn how to shape the world around us and bring things into being.

- *The High Priestess (Key 2).* The High Priestess represents the passive principle. She is the voice of the unconsciousness and the keeper of secrets. Through her we learn how to reflect, how to pay attention, and how to listen to our inner voice.

- *The Empress (Key 3).* The Empress represents the nurturant principle, the Earth Mother. From her all things are born, and she loves all of her children equally. She teaches us how to create ideas, nurture them, and eventually give birth to them in the form of concrete accomplishments.

- *The Emperor (Key 4).* The Emperor represents the Father, the patriarch. Through him we learn the rules, structure, and authority. We come to know boundaries: how to both abide by and create them. The Emperor shows us order as it exists in the world, allowing us to make sense of our experiences.

- *The Hierophant (Key 5).* Through the Hierophant, we learn the beliefs and traditions of our culture. We come to know what it means to be a part of a group. We are exposed to formal education. Spiritual orthodoxy, standards of ethics, and morality are all a part of the lessons that the Hierophant imparts.

- *The Lovers (Key 6).* The Lovers teach us to look outside ourselves to bring perspective to our lives. This perspective comes in the form of relationships. We learn how to relate to others in friendships and sexual unions. We may also have to make difficult choices at this stage. To do this, we must develop our own beliefs and values.

- *The Chariot (Key 7).* The Chariot depicts the Warrior, the Hero. At this stage, we learn how to face challenges head-on. Through discipline, exertion, and will, we learn how to overcome obstacles.

- *Strength (Key 8).* Through Strength, we learn how to develop our courage and resolve. Our lives will inevitably involve disillusionment and setbacks. The lessons of Strength teach us how to cope. We also learn how to balance the willful energy of the Chariot with the softer attributes of patience, kindness, and tolerance.

- *The Hermit (Key 9).* The Hermit represents the soul seeker who looks inward for enlightenment. He teaches us how to search ourselves for the deeper truths in our lives. The Hermit also imparts the need for quiet solitude away from the distractions of the world.

- *The Wheel Of Fortune (Key 10).* The Wheel teaches us about life's cycles and interconnectedness. We learn that life is a cycle of ups, downs, and turning points. Seemingly random events may be a part of life's larger patterns.

- *Justice (Key 11)*. Justice shows us the meaning of cause and effect: that what we do in our lives has outcomes and consequences, and we must take responsibility for them. Through Justice, we also learn how to show fairness towards others and how to live within our limits.
- *The Hanged Man (Key 12)*. The Hanged Man teaches us about sacrifice, release, and letting go. At this stage, we learn that sometimes the best course of action is no course of action at all.
- *Death (Key 13)*. Through Death, we learn that sweeping, powerful change in our lives can be liberating and healthy. Scary and painful times can actually be times of the greatest opportunity. Death teaches us to accept and embrace the changes in our lives — not fear them.
- *Temperance (Key 14)*. Balance and moderation are the key lessons of Temperance. We learn how to mitigate extremes to find a harmonious middle ground and how to combine opposites into a centered whole.
- *The Devil (Key 15)*. The Devil brings us face to face with the obstacles and limitations we place on ourselves through our own fear, ignorance, and greed. We learn that the restrictions we perceive are often the result of our own habits of thought. By becoming conscious of our limiting beliefs, we can move past them and grow.
- *The Tower (Key 16)*. The lessons of the Tower can be painful. Sudden, dramatic, and often unexpected events are a part of these lessons. But upheavals can bring revelations of new knowledge, experience, and, ultimately, wisdom.
- *The Star (Key 17)*. After the upsets of the Tower, the Star teaches us how to heal. We learn how to pull ourselves

back together after experiencing inner turmoil. The Star brings peace, calm, and a renewed sense of optimism.

- *The Moon (Key 18)*. Through the Moon, we learn how to tap into our unconscious to discover hidden emotions and dreams. Along the way, we discover that things are not always as they appear to be. We learn how to see through the illusions and access the deepest parts of ourselves.

- *The Sun (Key 19)*. The Sun shows us that we are truly great and that we can radiate that greatness outward to help others. We come to know confidence, pride, and self-worth.

- *Judgment (Key 20)*. When we reach Judgment, we learn our true vocation, that which calls to us most deeply in this life. We also learn how to forgive ourselves for past mistakes and start again anew.

- *The World (Key 21)*. When we have reached the World, we have integrated the disparate parts of ourselves and have achieved wholeness. Having completed one cycle, we are ready to begin again, as Fools.

2. The Quartered Circle

The Quartered Circle is an important symbol for Wiccans and many other Pagans. It's really a complex cluster of symbols. To me, it speaks of a harmonious diversity, a wholeness that is comprised of parts that fit and work together well. The circle is unity; the quarters are the diverse component parts.

Each quarter anchors a variety of assigned meanings, called *correspondences*. These begin with the four alchemical elements: air, fire, water, and earth. The quarters are also associated with colors, animals, seasons, and more. The most important set of correspondences for our purpose includes the four basic ways that humans interact with their surroundings. Secular psychologists will recognize these as the classic Jungian Quaternity of cognition, emotion, intuition, and sensation. I prefer plainer and less confusing terms: thought, passion, wisdom, and skill.

We all need all of these, but not necessarily in constant and perfect four-way balance. Different people have different strengths and styles. Different situations call for different approaches. The balance we need is dynamic, constantly shifting, an inner dance of mind, heart, and spirit.

Our culture tends to favor airy intellect and earthy skill, to the detriment of passion or intuition. Most of us were trained from childhood in that unbalanced manner. This has harmed us, individually and collectively, and has brought great harm to Mother Earth. Some of us are disgusted and frightened. We are tempted to overcompensate.

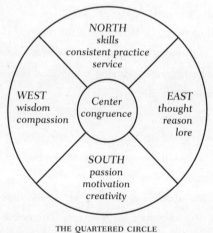

THE QUARTERED CIRCLE

Spirituality seems to be born of water, flowing from the wellsprings, nurturing the roots. The techniques of spiritual quest — meditation, ritual, dream work, divination — are all associated with the West. The people we perceive as spiritual, as advanced on the path, are insightful, compassionate, wise — and completely out of synch with the driven and insensitive commercial culture that surrounds us.

I think this very dramatic contrast fools us into overemphasizing the intuitive function.

All four functions are necessary, all are good — and all can be harmful if exaggerated or unbalanced. Just as some care and compassion would improve the business world, a bit of rational caution would serve us well in our quest for Spirit. You can, and should, get into your heart without getting out of your head. They are not opposed, not even in the sense of a polarity. Each enriches the other.

The diagram above shows how I think all four functions contribute to spiritual development. Here are some additional thoughts:

- *East/Air/Thought/Evidence and Logic/Lore*. In this quarter we place all codified knowledge, both from our Pagan predecessors and contemporaries and from non-Pagan scholars. There is so much to learn. To this quarter we bring our capacity for critical thinking, our willingness to weigh received wisdom from any source against other perspectives and, most important, against our own experience. Rationality guards us from superstition and fundamentalism.
- *South/Fire/Passion and Drive/Will*. In this quarter we place energy and motivation. Here thought and inspiration gain potency. To this quarter we bring self-examination. What do I really want, from life and from the path? How much do I want it? How much of my time and energy can I realistically commit? Most important: Why? Without energy and will, inspiration stagnates.
- *West/Water/Wisdom and Compassion/Intuition*. In this quarter we place spirituality itself. To this quarter, we bring love and longing, the roots that reach down to the hidden water.

We are like desert plants: tough and hardy, well able to survive long droughts. We cannot bloom till the rains come. Knowledge without compassion is alienation.

- *North/Earth/Skill and Stability/Form.* In this quarter we place all that is physical and practical. Here potential takes form. Invisible love clothes itself in kindness and so becomes visible beauty. Here inspiration is made real through hours of consistent effort. Northern altars look very much like computer keyboards, drawing tables, cutting boards — the places where we make it happen. Spirituality must flow into service or it soon becomes smug and irrelevant. To this quarter, we must bring sensitivity, respect, and care, lest service become self-righteous meddling. Belief without action is hypocrisy.

- *Center/Magic/Balance and Integration/Responsibility.* In the Center we place ourselves and from the Center we experience and act, drawing on the strengths of all four quarters as needed, meeting the joys and challenges of life and of the path.

3. The Shaman's Journey

Shamans are "technicians of the sacred," specialists who trance and dream on behalf of the community.[16] Although the word *shaman* comes from Siberia, similar practitioners are found just about every place where indigenous people have managed to preserve their native religions and lifeways. The understanding of how one becomes a shaman differs from one group to another, but here's a sort of composite sequence that fits most of them pretty well:[17]

1. *Innocence.* Comparable to Rambo's *Context*, this is the starting point. It is a person, usually young, engaged in the ordinary daily life of the community.

2. *Call.* In some communities, all youngsters undertake a vision quest as an initiation to adulthood. Some of the visions they receive indicate a shamanic calling. In other communities, the role of shaman is inherited through families, or passed through apprenticeship at the elder shaman's invitation. In still others, the call comes from the Spirit World in the form of a sudden, usually severe, illness. Shamanic threshold illness is probably a form of spiritual emergency. This is comparable to Rambo's *Crisis*, except that it leads to a central role within the same religion, rather than to a change of religion.

3. *Training.* The elder teaches the apprentice lore and skills, exposing them to a variety of traditional learning experiences, some of which are challenges, ordeals, tests of ability or will.

4. *Empowerment.* By overcoming these challenges and ordeals, the trainee becomes confident and also forms relationships with various spirits, receiving their gifts of knowledge and power.

5. *Emergence and Celebration.* The elder announces to the community that the trainee is now fully qualified as a shaman. Often there is a ritual in which the new shaman's capacities are displayed, followed by a feast and celebration.

6. *Living in Accordance.* The new shaman will undertake certain ongoing responsibilities to the spirits, perhaps maintaining a shrine or following a particular diet. By serving the spirits, keeping that relationship active, they continue to receive the power to serve the community.

NAVIGATIONAL STARS

This chapter has described goals that we will never entirely reach. Have I written a lot of idealistic nonsense? Worse, am I some kind of pompous hypocrite, advocating to you what I know I have not myself achieved?

I have done things I ought not to have done. I have left undone things that I ought to have done. So have you. Does this mean there is no health in us, that whatever is imperfect is utterly worthless? Some of us were taught exactly that as children.

Or does it mean that ideals are sticks to beat ourselves with, that we should stop "shoulding on ourselves"? Should the only limit on hedonism be prudence, or maybe some long-term strategic planning for greater hedonism later on? Should other people — or other life forms — be regarded merely as assets or liabilities, without regard for their well-being, their Sacred value? Should we find virtue in selfishness and take "do what you will" as the whole of the law?

There is a third possibility. Unattainable ideals can serve us as navigational stars. We can steer by them with no expectation of ever reaching them and no recrimination when we get, instead, to where we were really going: to a good life, with close family and friends, a real sense of accomplishment, creative self-expression, and Sacred Contact.

Each of us must decide where we want to go, study the charts and the stars, choose which stars to steer by, watch out for storms and icebergs, and hold steady to our course. But personal does not have to mean eccentric or idiosyncratic. Autonomous does not have to mean isolated. Collective experience can be a resource instead of a restraint.

Talk with your own elders. Find out what is customary in your particular lineage or Tradition. Talk with people whose spirituality and wisdom you respect, whether they are Pagans or not. Read a lot more books than this one. Remember that all of these are maps, abstractions, subjective descriptions of a metaphoric territory. Don't assume that any one of them will perfectly fill your needs or those of your students.

Compare them against your own experience. Think about them carefully and critically. Try to identify places where they seem to describe the same landmark, even if in different words — those are the major features that are meaningful to just about every traveler. Meditate and dream with them and see how your deep mind responds.

Draw your own map. Even then, stay modest and tentative. Your own further adventures will teach you more about the territory. Features you barely noticed will be important markers for some student of yours. You will redraw that map again and again as you and your students explore the inner realms.

Although stable landmarks are easier to recognize, describe, or map, they are not the only important ones. I may learn endurance from a cliff face, yes. I may also learn about transformation and continuity from a nurse log or glory from the sunlight on a butterfly's wing.

As we walk the path and guide others, we need to pay attention, to notice, to understand, to enjoy.

TO LEARN MORE

Most of the readings I would recommend are listed in the notes for this chapter. I want to add just one more:

Young-Eisendrath, Polly and Melvin E. Miller, eds. *The Psychology of Mature Spirituality: Integrity, Wisdom, Transcendence.* London: Routledge, 2000. ISBN 0415179602

NOTES

[1] Samuel M. Natale, "Confrontation and the Religious Beliefs of a

Client," in *Psychotherapy and the Religiously Committed Patient*, ed. E. Mark Stern (New York: Haworth, 1985), 107–16.

[2] For more on Erikson's stage theory, see Erik H. Erikson, ed., *Adulthood* (New York: Norton, 1978) [most important]; Erik H. Erikson, *Identity and the Life Cycle* (New York: Norton, 1959); Erik H. Erikson, *The Life Cycle Completed* (New York: Norton, 1982); and Erik H. Erikson et al., *Vital Involvement in Old Age* (New York: Norton, 1986).

[3] For more on Maslow's theories, see A.H. Maslow, *Motivation and Personality* (New York: Harper & Row, 1970); A.H. Malsow, *Toward a Psychology of Being* (New York: Van Nostrand Reinhold, 1968); and A.H. Maslow, *The Further Reaches of Human Nature* (New York: Viking, 1971).

[4] Lewis R. Rambo, *Understanding Religious Conversion* (New Haven: Yale University Press, 1993).

[5] See <www.draknet.com/proteus>.

[6] Rambo calls this last stage *Consequences*, but I think a more neutral term works better. Consequences implies punishments or other bad outcomes, but some outcomes are very happy indeed.

[7] For more about this deeper understanding of faith, see Paul Tillich, *The Dynamics of Faith* (New York: HarperPerennial, 2001). This book, originally published in 1958, was the very first book our college chaplain invited us to read and discuss, my introduction to contemporary theology.

[8] James W. Fowler, *Stages of Faith* (San Francisco: HarperSanFrancisco, 1981).

[9] Ibid., 294.

[10] Some authoritarian groups may be honest, fair, and kindly, but others are nothing of the kind. Either way, authoritarian groups tend to stunt their members' growth. Isaac Bonewits has created a method for evaluating groups. You can find it in my first book, *Wicca Covens* (Citadel, 1999), 55–59 or in many different places on the Web, including the Proteus Coven Web site, <www.draknet.com/proteus/ABCDEF.HTML>.

[11] Maria Escudero, personal correspondence with author, 4 Jan. 2002.

[12] Rambo, *Understanding Religious Conversion*, 50.

[13] For more on this subject, see Martin E. P. Seligman, *What You Can Change and What You Can't* (New York: Fawcett Columbine, 1993).

[14] For full and deep correlation of psychological growth with the three-degree system of British Traditional Wicca, see Vivianne Crowley, *Wicca: The Old Religion in the New Millennium* (London: Thorsons, 1996). Dr. Crowley is both a qualified Jungian psychotherapist and a Traditional High Priestess.

[15] For a book-length account of the Fool's Journey, see Sallie Nichols, *Jung and Tarot: An Archetypal Journey* (New York: Weiser, 1980).

[16] There are many good books about shamanism. The one I find

most accessible and useful for practitioners is *Shamanism as a Spiritual Practice for Daily Life* by Tom Cowan (Freedom: Crossing Press, 1997). If you are drawn to Celtic culture, as many neo-Pagans are, I also recommend Cowan's earlier book, *Fire in the Head: Shamanism and the Celtic Spirit* (San Francisco: HarperSanFrancisco, 1993).

[17] The shaman's journey is parallel to the mythic "hero's journey." The classic description of the hero's quest is Joseph Campbell's book, *The Hero with a Thousand Faces* (New York: MJF Books, 1996).

Deity

CHAPTER 5

SEEKING CLOSENESS

RELIGION MEANS RECONNECTION, THE RE-ESTABLISHMENT
of a link that has been weakened or broken. The primary concern
of religion is the connection between humans and Deity. To be
sure, at the most basic level this link cannot be broken, but our
awareness of it, our conscious connection with Deity, can indeed
deteriorate or completely disappear. *Effective* religious activity
helps us to restore our awareness of our bond with the Ancient
Gods and to reclaim our functional access to Spirit.

Spirituality is the link, the connection itself. Religion serves
and supports spirituality. Pagan religion helps each of us recover
and keep the relationship we desire with the Ancient Gods of
Nature. Pagan religion, like any other religion, does this by two
major means: community and lore. Through religious participation, we join a group of like-minded people who will support our
quest. We also benefit from the work of many more people,
including those from other times and places. The Gods, the
community, and the lore: picture them as a triangle with the
Gods at the apex, the community and the lore at the base.

A mentor who works within a religious community — as
each Pagan mentor does — helps students connect with all
three points of that triangle. Add two more points to the figure
for mentor and seeker. Making a proper introduction between
two parties requires knowing them both. So each point must
connect to all four of the others. When you draw a diagram
showing all these interconnections, you get a very familiar
form.

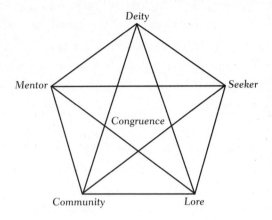

Deity

Mentor

Seeker

Congruence

Community

Lore

FIVE-SIDED MODEL OF RELIGIOUS PARTICIPATION

Energy flows along each of these lines in both directions. In later chapters, we will explore how a mentor can facilitate a student's connection with community and with lore. This chapter is about the most important of these links: that which joins the Pagan and the Entheoi.

William James was one of the first to study the psychology of religion. In 1902, in his great classic, *The Varieties of Religious Experience*, he gives this definition of religious conversion: "To say that a man is 'converted' means . . . that religious ideas, previously peripheral in his consciousness, now take a central place, and that religious aims form the habitual centre of his energy."[1] Notice that James is talking about a change of intensity or focus, not a change of religious affiliation.

This chapter is not about change of religious affiliation — that topic is discussed in the previous chapter. Neither is this chapter about becoming a priest/ess, claiming the honor and the obligation of Sacred service. Some of that is in Chapter 6, and there is more about it in my earlier book, *Wicca Covens*.[2]

This chapter is for and about James's sort of converts: people who already identify themselves as Pagan, who approach the Sacred through Pagan models and metaphors, and who now want a closer connection with the Ancient Gods. This chapter is about us becoming mystics, specifically Pagan nature mystics. It's about panentheistic mysticism, living connection with the Entheoi. This involves:

- becoming closer to the Ancient Gods of Nature;
- creating, deepening, clarifying, and sustaining conscious contact with Them;
- opening to Their guidance, inspiration, and power, to the energy that we call awen; and
- living our lives in congruence with that flow.

The most direct approach to nature mysticism is also the easiest: simple appreciation. The Entheoi are within us and all around us, pervading all that is. All we need to do, really, is become aware of Their Presence. Start with these two very simple things:

- Grace at meals. You don't even need words. Just pause for a moment to look at, smell, appreciate your food, and give silent thanks to Mother Earth and to all the plants, animals, and people that contributed to the meal. If a group is eating together, you may find that a simple statement of thanks helps you join your hearts in gratitude. Gratitude is the key.
- Greeting. When you leave your house in the morning, greet the first living thing you see: a tree, a cat, a pigeon, the grass that grows through the cracks in the pavement. Again, just a moment of silent appreciation is plenty.

    Greet the moon every evening in the same way. Kiss your hand to Her. That one simple thing, consistently done, will change your life.[3]

I'm suggesting that each of us, mentors and students alike, *intentionally* take a few moments every day for appreciation. That simply means we'll do it more often than others do. Everybody occasionally just stops to watch a child play or to listen to some lovely music. To notice and enjoy is to appreciate. So the practice of gratitude is itself a pleasure, and self-reinforcing. Every time we do it, we incline ourselves to do more, building a delightful habit. And here's the secret, the really big secret at the heart of this book, at the heart of nature mysticism: every time we do it, we open ourselves to ecstasy.

PEAK EXPERIENCES: THE GIFT

Read this: "The mother examining in loving ecstasy her new-born infant may be enthralled by every single part of him, one part as much as another one, one little toenail as much as another little toenail, and be struck into a kind of religious awe in this way."[4] The same thing can happen when somebody gets a mouthful of juicy ripe tomato, or sees the bright forsythia in the spring, or settles into a warm, scented bath. All it takes is attention and gratitude. Ours is a path of delight. All acts of love and pleasure really are our rituals.

That description of a mother enjoying her baby came from Abraham Maslow, the humanistic psychologist whose model of sequential needs we considered in the previous chapter. In his studies of self-actualizing people, Maslow found that many of them reported having had joyful moments of overwhelming "religious awe."

Maslow was an atheist, but as a good and honest scientist he was faithful to his observations. What he did was tease out the common features of what he called "peak-experiences" from these reports and compile a purely experiential description, without reference to Deity or theology. Here are some of the features Maslow identified:[5]

- perception of the universe as an integrated and unified whole
- relaxed but complete attention
- an absence of judgment or evaluation; a willingness to let be
- disorientation in time and space; a sense of eternity
- the perception that peak experiences give meaning to life
- the sense of the pervading goodness and beauty of the world; wonder, awe, reverence, gratitude
- resolution of apparent dichotomies or polarities
- the sense that one has been changed for the better and has become freer, more creative, more authentic

Maslow's composite description of peak experiences reveals what I would call a flash of awareness of Sacred Contact, the loving touch of the Entheoi. Our culture has trained us to hide this from ourselves, depriving us of something as natural and normal as water. As Maslow put it, "I finally began to use the word 'non-peaker' to describe, not the person who is unable to have peak-experiences, but rather the person who is afraid of them, who suppresses them, who denies them, who turns them away, or who 'forgets' them."[6]

All of us are seekers. Sacred Contact is what we seek. Some of us are mentors. Sacred Contact is what we help people find.

Receiving the Gift

The Gods offer free gifts. Some people are more receptive than others. Some people intentionally seek such gifts. Some just seem to stumble into them, without conscious effort, without even knowing there was something worth seeking. Some people believe that any such quest is futile because we are insignificant and powerless before the Gods. Some believe that quest is super-fluous because the gift is already given. We will find the awen we seek within ourselves. The Entheoi have been with us from the beginning and will remain until the end of days.

Here's what I think: Although we participate in Deity, we cannot change Deity. The part cannot change the whole. We can neither control Deity nor force Deity to give us anything. The only thing we can control or change is ourselves, our consciousness, the focus of our attention.

History and experience show that we can decline the gift, shut out the awareness, rip the web of empathy that links us to the Sacred and to all that lives. If we can decline the gift, we can also choose to accept it with thanks. We can alter our consciousness in accordance with will. Indeed, this is one of the two classic defi-nitions of magic. Perhaps we can only do this because the Gods allow us the option. It doesn't matter. Here and now, our beliefs, choices, and behaviors make the difference.

We have choices. As always, choice brings responsibility. We can actively seek Contact, or passively await it, or ignore it altogether. We can prepare ourselves to receive the awen, but nothing forces us to prepare. If we choose to seek or to prepare, we know of a wide range of techniques, drawn from many different times, places, and cultures. We can begin to assess the effectiveness of these techniques and their compatibility with our values, our path, our understandings of Deity. Mentors should be specialists in consciousness-altering techniques, be able to use them with skill, and gauge which will be most helpful to any particular student. Here's a very simple prelimi-nary sort:

Change of Consciousness: Four Approaches

	PREPARED	UNPREPARED
Sought	Quest • meditation • trance work	Risk • recreational drugs
Unsought	Surprise • simple gratitude • exoteric religious activity	Crisis • ergotism • shamanic threshold illness

Any group of elders could come up with many more examples to place in each of the table's four cells. The few presented there are just the first instances that occurred to me, not a complete list. I want to share a few thoughts about these four groupings.

Quest (prepared and sought)

Intentional seekers are the ones most likely to ask a mentor for guidance. Typically, they are young adults who are headed for clergy roles or mature adults who want to deepen their spiritual connections. Self-aware seekers are able to prepare themselves to receive the gift they seek.

Preparation, for this purpose, means general maturity and readiness, as discussed in Chapter 4, *plus* appropriate set and setting. (*Set* is short for *mindset*, meaning expectation, internal preparation. *Setting* means the physical context, external preparation.) Maturity and readiness develop over a lifetime. Set and setting, with practice, can be established in less than an hour, sometimes in seconds.

Surprise (prepared but unsought)

This is the epiphany that surprises us with joy when we suddenly find the Sacred in a lover's eyes or in the reverent, soaring voices of a choir.

People can open themselves to awe and wonder by participating in the arts, or contemplating nature, or watching babies learn to walk. Remember, many of Maslow's self-actualizers reported peak experiences even if they were not religious practitioners and did not ascribe those moments to the movement of Deity.

Religious people prepare by engaging in the exoteric, lay practice of their religion. They go to services, read scriptures, pray. All this cultivates a sense of closeness with Deity. It also establishes a mindset in which Sacred encounter, if and when it comes, will probably be interpreted according to that religion's values, myths, and symbols.

Paganism is no different. Participation in rituals that celebrate the beauty of the green earth and the white moon among the stars will predispose us to find the Sacred in nature, and to perceive the God/desses and spirits of nature in our own moments of epiphany.

Any such surprise gift from Deity is an invitation to mysticism. The thing is, such invitations are really widely distributed. Deity does not play favorites. In Pagan terms, Mother Earth loves all Her children equally.

Many people lack the inclination or the time and energy to respond. Some people — mostly those who are comfortable with their identities, stable and content with love and work, moving into personal self-actualization and reflective faith — will want to accept the invitation. These people will shift to quest mode and begin making intentional and active efforts to create, deepen, clarify, and sustain conscious contact with the Entheoi. As part of this, they may enter one of the structured traditions or seek personal mentoring.

Risk (sought but unprepared)

This is a danger zone. When altered states of consciousness are sought without proper preparation, the seeker risks painful disorientation. Think, for example, of people who take mind-altering drugs when they are already upset about something, or who take such drugs in unsafe surroundings. The drugs amplify emotional sensitivity, so a bad trip is almost guaranteed. The ritual use of entheogens, with appropriate set and setting, brings a very different result.

Pathological preparation, which is worse than none at all, engenders an even more severe risk. If a person in a receptive state is consistently exposed to violent, brutal inputs, such as hell-fire preaching or images of tortured saints, it's not surprising that they would impose those images onto whatever inflow of energy they experience. Hateful fanaticism — crusade, pogrom, and jihad — is the logical outcome. Mind as well as body, we are what we eat.

Please notice that all the same problems can arise when people enter deep meditative or trance states without proper preparation. It's even possible for people to get addicted to meditation, doing so much of it that they leave no time for normal life chores or using it as a way to evade their problems. Maturity, set, and setting are what make the difference — not the means by which consciousness is altered.

Are you, as a Pagan mentor, likely to encounter people with this sort of problem? Yes. Consider the high-profile weekend intensive workshop. Few, if any, assess participants for readiness. They may engage in deep exploratory practices that open up painful old issues that had been deeply buried. This is necessary to clear the channel for the flow of awen. But work like this takes more than a weekend. Some participants may not be ready to face what is revealed. They may not be well connected with a local community that can support them as they work through these memories and issues. When the weekend ends, they are left stranded with the aftermath.

If they find their way to you, what can you do? Help them stabilize and ground. Make sure they eat and sleep. When they are stable, help them understand what happened. Urge them not to swing from trapezes like this again before they've installed a safety net. Help them find a good counselor or therapist. Know that the ultimate responsibility is theirs. You cannot and should not force them to follow your advice.

Crisis (unsought and unprepared)

From the thirteenth through the seventeenth centuries, a number of episodes of dancing mania, called *tarantism*, hit rural Europe. Those afflicted believed they had been driven crazy by the poisonous bite of the tarantula spider. This is the origin of the folk dance called the *tarantella*. But later research offers a different hypothesis: convulsive ergotism.

Ergot is a fungus that lives on grain, usually rye. It produces a mind-altering alkaloid that is closely related to LSD. The symptoms of convulsive ergotism include itching and tingling, vertigo, distorted perception, hallucinations, and delirium, as well as convulsions. Whole villages were inadvertently "dosed" with a psychedelic drug in their rye bread, and driven to dance. People were completely unprepared when these drug-induced symptoms hit. They had no idea what was happening to them and no notion of how to take care of themselves or each other.

Shamanic threshold illness is another example of an overwhelming and unsought alteration of consciousness, a spiritual emergency for which the person is not prepared. But, in indigenous communities, the culture *is* prepared. A supportive setting exists even if the anticipatory mindset did not. Elders will recognize the symptoms and guide the afflicted person to a new and valued role in the community. Crisis, properly managed, becomes opportunity.

As Pagan mentors, are we likely to encounter people in this sort of chaotic crisis? Yes. Consider the unprepared college kid, turning up at a large festival looking for nothing more than a wild weekend, maybe alone and certainly clueless. Then they find themselves alone in a crowd at a high-intensity fire circle with trance drumming and trance dancing, the strobe effect of a bonfire, their defenses lowered by fatigue. The inner dam breaks, and awen rushes in. Depending on their upbringing, this may all be complicated by guilt or even by real fear if we are the people their parents warned them about. This person may not yet have a stable identity in life. They are in unfamiliar surroundings that feel — and might actually be — unsafe. They have no reason to expect what they experience and no opportunity to prepare them-selves for it. It's no wonder if they react by panicking.

We may be able to help some of them turn this crisis into an opportunity, an invitation to explore the inner paths, to find a better way to receive and channel the awen. I'll be discussing spiritual emergency at length later on in this chapter.

DEITY: GENERAL CONCEPTS

The peak experience, however it comes, can be taken as an invi-tation to a closer relationship with Deity. Mentors may be asked to help develop this relationship. The next question is this: to whom are we introducing our students? This is not as simple a question as it might seem. According to the understandings of panentheism, the Sacred pervades all the universe — and more. Each of us is a part of Deity, linked to all else from the very center of our being. The Entheoi can and do move within everyone's core. How can we define anything so all-pervading and so huge?

From Margarian Bridger and Stephen Hergest, teaching elders in Calgary, comes the very important insight that there are three main concepts of Deity prevalent among Pagans. They propose that these three concepts can form the endpoints of a triangle, and that we can arbitrarily assign a color to each point. Just as colors can blend, the three concepts can shade into each other. People can place themselves anywhere within the triangle's area. Here's their description of the three ways of understanding Deity:

- **Red**. The first of these endpoints is the orthodox deist position: the gods are personal, named, individual entities with whom one can communicate almost as one would with human beings. They may or may not be humanlike. They exist in a way ("level", "plane", or "dimension") that is far beyond human comprehension, but their existence is objectively verifiable.
- **Blue**. Deity exists. It is the Ultimate Sacred/Great Mystery/Source. It is so great, so subtle, so all-encompassing, that we cannot hope to comprehend more than a tiny fraction of it. Being ourselves human, we relate best to things that are humanlike, and so we have "the gods": humanlike metaphors or masks that we place upon the faceless Face of the Ultimate, so that through them we can perceive and relate to a little of It.
- **Yellow**. The gods exist only as constructs within the human mind and imagination. They are Truths — valid ways of making sense out of human thought and experience, personifications of abstracts that might otherwise be too slippery for the human mind to grasp — but they are not Facts; they have no objectively verifiable existence. Like other abstracts (e.g. Freedom, Democracy, Love, Truth), they enrich our lives and

are worth believing in, but it is naive to think that they have any objectively verifiable existence. It doesn't matter that the gods aren't factual; they're true, and that's what's important.[7]

You can use this model of a triangle with blended colors as the basis for an exercise in self- (or group) exploration.

WHAT COLOR IS YOUR DEITY CONCEPT?

We may assume that we know what a god or goddess is, but different people have different understandings, and these understandings seem to vary with the circumstances in which we find ourselves. This exercise facilitates awareness of our own theological concepts, the guiding assumptions with which we approach Deity.

If you're using this exercise with students, first do it yourself. Then explain the three concepts to your students. That can be the springboard to a very interesting and instructive discussion, even before you ask them to place themselves on the triangle.

On a sheet of paper, draw an outline of an equilateral triangle, then color it in. Make one point red, one blue, and one yellow. Blend the colors smoothly through the triangle's area. Watercolors work well for this because they blend so easily.

After the paper is dry, date the place where you feel you belong right now. Remember that no location within the triangle is holier or more accurate than any other; anywhere you place yourself is okay. Keep this sheet in your journal. Record your position again periodically, perhaps once a month. Notice how much your perceptions change over time. Try to identify the reasons for your changes.

The triangle can also be the basis for a group bonding exercise. Explain and discuss the three concepts of Deity. Pass a colored triangle around the circle. Ask each member to initial their current position and explain it to the group. They will learn about themselves, and also learn that people with quite different concepts of Deity can work well together in a Pagan spiritual group. Free people have no need for dogma.

Insofar as we are living, learning, and growing, our concepts of Deity will change over time, which changes our positions within the triangle. It's easy to understand the slow gradual changes that accompany individual development. I suspect that people in Fowler's synthetic-conventional stage of faith generally tend to hold red concepts of deity. Yellow concepts prevail among those in Fowler's individuative-reflective stage, and blue concepts in his conjunctive stage.

But color me purple, and iridescent at that. My shading changes according to the need of the moment. I'm deep cobalt blue while sitting at a computer screen or having a philosophical discussion with friends over a good meal. That's my way of thinking about the Gods, but it's not how I relate with them. To actually interact with Deity, I shift towards red. In formal ritual, I go all the way to the red corner.

At the start of our rites, we ground, center, set aside trivial distractions, and focus ourselves on the Sacred and on the work at hand. I suggest that, for those of us who are not full-time reds, a large part of what we mean by focusing on the Sacred is shifting to the red end of the spectrum. Photographers might understand this as more like changing the filter than the focus.

In "red consciousness," the Gods are real entities with whom we can interact. Maybe the Ineffable takes the form of specific

Gods in order to interact with us. Maybe we build models through which the Ineffable graciously communicates. I don't presume to know what "really" happens, but I am very sure it works.

Based on my own experience, I think that people can move freely within the triangle, working from whatever concepts of Deity work best for the situation they are in, and for the needs of the moment. That's why there are "no atheists in foxholes." In crisis, we don't want to philosophize — we want to latch on!

We can make these shifts because all these concepts and more are True, just as they all are incomplete. Deity is bigger than the sum of all our concepts and constructs, all our models and metaphors, because Deity is bigger than the collective group mind of all of humankind. No human concept can hold Deity, nor should any one concept of Deity capture us.

The shift to red, what theater folks call the "willed suspension of disbelief," is absolutely necessary for any kind of religious ritual or practice to work. But nobody can make such a shift until they understand that there are different concepts, and that moving among them is possible.

Mentors need to make sure students know this, and teach them how to do it. But our concept of Deity is not trivial. How can we make a deliberate shift in something so important? By magic, of course; by the art of changing consciousness in accordance with will. We can help each other build this skill by the practice of active imagination.

PRACTICING ACTIVE IMAGINATION

To imagine is to create a mental image of something that is not immediately present to your senses. That includes the Gods, of course, but is not limited to Them. For practice, I suggest you work with mental images that are playful and fun, like these:

- A picnic. What are you bringing? Not just food, but books, musical instruments, sports equipment, a camera. Describe what you would enjoy having with you for an afternoon in the country. How do you get there? What is it like? What do you do?
- You sense another presence in the room, perhaps a ghost. There's no feeling of hostility or fear, but maybe something more like curiosity or care. Do you see anything, feel a change of atmosphere, hear or smell anything? What hints to you that another personality is there? Do you get any sense of who this is: a relative, a former occupant of the room?
- A friendly talking fish is swimming around in the air of your room at about shoulder height. What is it saying? Does it give you a small kiss on the cheek?
- Each participant in the exercise is astride a flying horse. What do you see as you fly across the area side by side?

You can certainly create your own exercises. Use anything that would be enjoyable for you and your student. One key is that you both (or all, if it's a group) enter into the picture, describing what you experience to each other, building on each other's descriptions. Another key — and this is very important — is that you do not limit yourselves to visual descriptions. Be sure to include hearing, taste, touch, and smell along with sight. The more senses you involve, the more vivid your image becomes for other people.

As you construct exercises for your students, please notice that the four I just offered follow a definite progression:

- The picnic is entirely possible in ordinary reality; it is just not happening at the moment.
- The ghost is not part of ordinary reality, but all you do is observe — you don't interact.
- You talk with, and probably touch, the fish; that is, you interact with it.
- You fly on the horse; you actively participate in the fantasy.

Some groups use fantasy role-playing games as training exercises because they strengthen the imagination and give people practice interacting with each other in imaginal situations.

For solitary practice, read fantasy literature. There's lots of good fantasy being written for adults these days. Some books even include Pagan Gods as characters. Read in comfortable leisure and build the images in your mind.

CULTIVATING PEAK EXPERIENCES

People who have learned how to make the shift to "red" consciousness are likely to interpret their peak experiences as Sacred Contact. Subject to all the complex issues we've been considering up to now, some of them will want more and ask you to help them work towards their own spiritual development, and towards having more, and more vivid, moments of conscious contact with the Entheoi.

For a farmer, cultivation means preparing and improving the soil to help the crops root, grow, and bear good fruit. For teachers, counselors, and clergy, it means forming, nurturing, fostering, and refining human development.

Spiritual mentors certainly converse with their students about spiritual interests and issues, but our role goes beyond that of a spiritually oriented counselor. We also, by the student's request and permission, create and present a series of experiences intended to nurture the student's growth, and to lead to direct encounters with the Ancient Gods, to epiphanies that culminate in gnosis. We hope to cultivate within each student their own direct relationship with the Entheoi.

The developmental experiences that we present should be congruent with our most central values and best understandings of Deity. They should also be effective and sequential. Each should build on the previous one, prepare for the next, and help open the student's awareness of the Entheoi.

Some of these experiences will be derived from your particular Tradition and also serve to foster the student's sense of connection with the community. People bond around common experiences. Others will be tailored to each particular student's background, temperament, and needs. Some will be as simple as asking the student to read a particular book and report on what they learned; others will be demanding vision quests or complicated rituals.

How can we help increase the frequency of peak experiences?

- For some, help them understand what that beautiful — but disorienting — experience they just had actually was. For others who already know what it was, help them identify other, similar experiences that they've had in the past.
- Help them identify what they were doing when Spirit touched them. Which of their behaviors, inner or outer, makes Contact more or less likely? How could they change their surroundings or actions to increase the possibility of Contact?
- Help them design a personal spiritual practice. Serve as their technical advisor, a person with expert knowledge of a range of spiritual practices. Educate yourself for this role in both the library and the lab.

- Present some experiences, such as the exercises in this book, within your working sessions and with your personal guidance.
- Help the student process and evaluate what happens when they try various things, so they can discover what works best for them. They will probably need to do some experimentation before settling in to a practice that is both effective and feasibly in balance with family, work, and play.
- Act as coach while they build the habits of consistent practice.
- Help them to interpret and integrate any results that they get and to apply these insights to their daily lives.
- Make sure they understand that changing life circumstances will occasionally direct further adjustments of their practice.

As their conscious contact with the Entheoi becomes active and stable in their lives, they will become less dependent on you and more reliant on that interaction. Then your job is done.

The Spiritual Toolbox: Some Basic Techniques

We live in a very different world from that of even our recent ancestors. One of the biggest differences is that we have access to much more information, more than any one of us could ever really use. Certainly this is the case with regard to spiritual practice. (That's one important reason for working in groups: each member can explore different aspects, thus widening everyone's scope.) We can learn practices from many different cultures and time periods.

Rather than trying to compile an encyclopedia, I want to present my personal "shortlist." These are practices I find basic to Paganism. I encourage you and your students to explore many, many other vehicles for the path — and to share your discoveries with the rest of us. Here are mine:[8]

Meditation

This is the most basic of all techniques, and the absolute prerequisite to the rest. Simply take a few moments every day for calm, still, inner listening. Thoughts will arise, and that's fine. Don't pursue them. Let them float past you like leaves in a stream.

Some people find that repeating a simple word or phrase (a mantra) helps calm the mind. Choose something with a lot of humming, resonant *m* and *n* sounds in it, like the classic *om*. Nonsense syllables, or words in languages you don't understand, can work. Carefully chosen words might also remind you to shift to red, increasing the probability of Sacred Contact. The perfect mantra for Goddess worshipers just might be *mama*.

You might also want to try counting your breaths. Just count one to four, and start again. Or you might use a natural or ritual object as a tactile and visual focus. Some people use a string of beads or a knotted cord, moving one bead or knot with each breath.

To learn a lot more about meditation, read *How to Meditate: A Guide to Self-Discovery* by Lawrence LeShan (Boston: Little Brown, 1999), ISBN 0316880620.

Journal Keeping

A personal journal is a way to track your own growth. A plain spiral notebook will work. A ring binder might work better if you want to make it a sort of scrapbook, including artwork or clippings as well as your writing. Record whatever seems related: books or articles you read and what you think about them, experiences during spiritual practice, random insights, questions that come to mind, and much more. Review it periodically, maybe at the dark moons. It will help you plan your next few steps.

To learn more about journal work, read *Life's Companion: Journal Writing as a Spiritual Quest* by Christina Baldwin, (New York: Bantam, 1991), ISBN 0553352024.

Dream Work

Traditions of dream work are as ancient as recorded history and as modern as contemporary psychology. Prepare by getting plenty of rest. We remember our dreams best when we sleep lightly. Keep a notebook or tape recorder by your bed. Record your dreams as soon as possible after waking. If you wake from a dream, record your impressions in the first person, present tense. If you wake with a feeling but no story, stay with the feeling and make up a story.

Interpret your dreams by your own free association rather than somebody else's definitions. If the dream suggests any artwork to you, make it and keep it near you. It may stimulate further associations or insights.

To learn more about dream work, read *The Variety of Dream Experience*, edited by Montague Ullman and Claire Limmer (Albany: SUNY Press, 1999), ISBN 079144256X or *Night and Day: Use the Power of Your Dreams to Transform Your Life* by Jack Maguire (New York: Simon and Schuster, 1989), ISBN 067165845X.

Nature Study

If we claim that our theological basis is reverence for Mother Earth and the natural cycles, it behooves us to learn a lot more about how those cycles operate in our own bioregion and to give more than lip service in these threatening times. Here are a few starting points:

- Spend time in the wilderness, or in your local park.
- Learn to identify local wildflowers, birds, or trees.
- Notice and appreciate the grass that grows through cracks in the sidewalk. Photograph or sketch the small natural beauties that we usually ignore, or write poetry or songs about them.

- If you have a yard, plant and care for a garden. Eat what you grow, and compost what you can to establish a conscious reciprocal relationship with the Earth (all life is such a reciprocal relationship, although often not consciously).
- Do what you can to support Mother Earth according to your own talents and temperaments, but the more directly the better. Volunteer at a local park. Show up for clean-up projects. Be careful about your own patterns of consumption and disposal. Protest any further environmental destruction. Write letters to legislators in support of environmental protection.

To learn more about our connection with nature, read Chas Clifton's essay "Nature Religion for Real," originally published in *Gnosis* 48 (Summer 1998), now available on the Proteus Coven Web site, <www.draknet.com/proteus/forreal.htm> and *A Sand County Almanac* by Aldo Leopold (New York: Oxford University Press, 2001), ISBN 0195146174. Or, best of all, get out of doors!

Art Work

Creative self-expression frees the flow of awen. To do this, you will need to learn a craft. Any craft will do: drawing, music, cooking, poetry, dance, etc. Even if you've never thought of yourself as an artist before, put some time and work into learning the skills. As your fluency increases, so will your accuracy and freedom of expression.

Don't worry if you never become a famous artist. The point is not to gain an adoring audience or build a professional career. What matters is that you place your personal creativity in the service of the Gods, the people, and the Earth.

You can get some good, sensible advice from *Freeing the Creative Spirit: Drawing on the Power of Art to Tap the Magic &*

Wisdom Within by Adriana Diaz (Toronto: HarperCollins, 1992), ISBN 0062507828. But the most important way to learn any craft is through hands-on practice.

Living in Accordance

This is the most important — and the most unglamorous — spiritual practice of all: just living every day on the basis of the values of our religion and the insights and guidance we receive from the Entheoi. Without this, all the rest is self-delusion and hypocrisy. Behavior is the only thing that matters. It is the proof of both faith and growth.

PERSONAL GOD/DESS INTENSIVE

As you become confident in your student's readiness, and your student becomes comfortable with these and other tools and techniques of spiritual exploration, they will probably want to create closer personal relationships with one or more particular Goddesses or Gods. Here's one way for them to do that:

1. Ask your student to choose any Goddess or God from any nation or time period. Is there a Deity they've felt drawn to for some time, or have even just been curious about? Or would they like to learn more about a particular culture or pantheon? Perhaps they want to choose a Deity who is related to things that are happening in their life right now, or goals they'd like to be working towards. Or let the Gods decide, and have the student pull a name out of a hat.

2. Have the student take a minimum of a month for research. Encourage them to find out all they can about this Deity's stories, symbols, favorite colors,

incenses, flowers, invocations, and poetry (both classical and contemporary) — anything they can find. It's a good idea to have them make a scrapbook of the material they collect.

3. Have them spend a second month at least using the information they discovered to work intensely with their chosen Deity. If possible, the student should set up an altar in their home, wear the Deity's symbolic colors, and eat the Deity's favorite foods or the typical cuisine of His or Her native culture. The student should meditate daily and engage in ritual as often as possible. In every way imaginable, the student should live in close contact with the Deity of their choice. They should celebrate the God/dess through their chosen art form and record the entire experience in their journal.

4. The student should share what they've learned with the community by writing an article, presenting a workshop at a gathering, or by any other means.

HINT: Encourage your student to do the research from a blue perspective, then have them shift to red when they are doing the month of intensive practice.

Trance Work

Pagan spiritual mentors and teachers often guide their students in trance. Trance is a safe and natural method for achieving altered states of consciousness in which we can much more easily interact with the Ancient Gods.

There's nothing unusual or exotic about the experience of trance. Have you ever been frightened in the movies, screaming futile warnings to the images on the screen? Become so involved with the book you were reading that you didn't hear people speak to you? Found yourself at work without remembering much of the trip there? Almost everyone has had such experiences, which means almost everyone has been in a variety of spontaneously occurring trances.

We are magic users. One of the classic definitions of magic is "The art of changing consciousness in accordance with will." An integral part of our magic, then, is that we enter trance *by choice*, and use trance to consciously explore our own inner worlds, and, through them, the Otherworld. To this end, we develop fluency in entering trance states, working within them, and returning fully and safely to ordinary waking consciousness.

However, up to now, few of us have received specific training in how to guide and facilitate trance for each other. It seems like plain common sense to add this skill to the mentor's toolbox.

Showing is better than telling for this. By far, the best and easiest way to learn trance facilitation skills is by direct observation followed by supervised practice. Find whatever opportunities you can for experiential learning. If that's unavailable to you, talk things over with trusted friends. The best feedback of all, of course, is your own thoughtful attention to your experiences working with trance. Here are some pointers to get you started.

Step by Step Guide to Trance-Working

You probably have one or more friends who are well-practiced meditators. Ask them to let you watch while they meditate. Take careful note of the visible, physical changes that take place. Observe their breath rate, skin coloring, postural and facial changes from reduced muscle tension, etc. These are the same changes to watch for when you are guiding someone into trance.

Start with the body. Trance work can involve sitting still for a relatively long period. People can do this more comfortably if they release as much overt muscular tension as possible before they begin. So, at minimum, ask them to stretch and shake out before settling down.

If the person you are guiding is a beginner, or if they seem particularly tense, you can do progressive deep muscle relaxation. This is a sort of self-massage, involving clenching and then suddenly relaxing various muscle groups. Work through the whole body. Be particularly sure to include the face. A whole lot of tension rides there, particularly for people who have to suppress their emotions or display emotions they don't particularly feel (as most of us do at work).

Whether or not you have done the deep muscle relaxation, have the person review their body, feel into each area in turn, and release any remaining tension.

Ground and center yourself. Keep your own breath slow and deep, your own muscles relaxed. Speak quietly, in a calm and soothing tone. You can't fake or "technique" this. Before you can calm others, you yourself need to be calm. Remember that the person (or group) you are guiding is entering a hyperreceptive state of consciousness. They will pick up on any residual tension, or any other incongruity, in you.

If you're working with a single person, you can track the rate of their breathing. A good way to do this is to slightly raise and lower your own hand as their belly raises and lowers with each breath. At first, match the cadence of your speech to their breath rate. After a while, very gradually, slow your speech. Their breath will slow down to match your phrasing. With a group, exaggerate your own breath, and gradually slow it along with your speech. They will probably follow along.

It's both more effective and more consistent with our beliefs to use the language of permission and invitation rather than the language of command. You might do this by saying something like,

"I invite you to get as relaxed and comfortable as you want to, as relaxed and comfortable as you feel is best for you, while still staying in touch with the sound of my voice."

Remind the person or group that the depth of their trance is entirely under their own control and that they can return to ordinary consciousness any time they want or need to. This is an important safety precaution for any trancer. Some will not be able to shift their consciousness at all without this explicit assurance that they have the right and power to leave trance at their own will.

The person(s) entering trance will begin to show the same physical changes that you saw in the meditator. Describe these changes as you see them. This will reinforce them and help deepen the trance. It's good to mix these descriptions with statements about the immediate environment: sounds, light conditions, temperature — whatever. Since these statements are obviously true, they lend credibility to your descriptions of the signs of deepening trance. If there are unpleasant noises or other potential irritants in your environment, be sure to acknowledge them, to weave them into the trance. Otherwise, they might become distractions. Also weave in statements about how the person is becoming increasingly relaxed and comfortable, and can become still more relaxed, just as relaxed as they choose, while remaining focused and receptive.

In later sessions, as trust develops and people become more fluent with trance, you can shorten some of the preliminaries. Perhaps a long staircase can turn into a funhouse slide. Eventually, with practice, you can just take a long, deep breath, say something like, "Remember what it feels like to be in trance," breathe deeply again, and people will enter trance.

There are several different potential purposes for entering this kind of relaxed and receptive state of consciousness. Here are three of the more common ones:

- *Self-management and/or self-improvement.* People may want to use trance to help mobilize inner resources for working towards some practical goal, such as stopping smoking, improving their athletic or musical performance, preparing for childbirth, or even stimulating their immune system.

- *Self-exploration.* Trance can facilitate encounters with power animals, spirit guides, ancestors, guardian angels, etc. These figures, which represent power and wisdom of many kinds, may engage the trancer in dialogue, offer them advice or gifts, take them on adventures within the Otherworld. Leave silent pauses in your facilitation to allow the trancer's active imagination space to work in. The change wrought in the person will be deeper and more pervasive, but less noticeable — the change involves a change in insight rather than a specific behavioral change.

- *Cultural or subcultural exploration.* In path-working, which is guided meditation within a Pagan religious context, we witness and experience the myths, the great teaching stories of our religion. Like dream narratives, these stories are always told in the present tense: you see, you hear, you do. Depending on the vividness of the experience, the person may participate in the action or merely witness it, but they never just hear about it. These experiences give people a deeper understanding of and connection with our Gods.

People encounter reality through several different *representational systems* based on different senses. Some of us are primarily visual, others primarily audial, still others primarily tactile and/or kinetic. What this means is that a charged ritual object will glow for some, hum for others, and be warm or vibrate to some other hands. So when working with an individual, you'll want to figure out which is their lead sense and couch your trance narrative primarily in those terms. With a group, be sure to include cues for all senses, so everyone can participate fully.

Use the language of direct experience as much as possible. Going into trance requires shifting to the red perspective, in which Otherworld persons and events are completely real for us. Avoid directions like "imagine" or "remember" once you are into the journey (although these can be useful for induction). Use the present tense and generally simple language and grammar. Avoid passive constructions, conditional forms, and the like. In trance we work with Younger Self, who is grammatically unsophisticated.

Use specific details if the symbolism is intrinsic to your work: particular colors, trees, animals, etc. may relate to particular Deities or energies. Other than that, leave as much scope as possible for your listeners' imaginations. More experienced travelers will need less guidance.

If you're going to specify, do so at once. Don't move from the general to the specific. If you say, "You are standing by the water's edge," and only later go on to describe a quiet lake, you will disorient participants who have created inner seashores or babbling mountain brooks.

You may place your listeners as participants or as observers, based on how intense an experience you feel they can handle. Take into account how experienced, strong, and adventurous they are and what kind of experience you are planning to present. People who can happily join the Maiden in a May Dance might still do better to simply watch the Wild Hunt go by rather than riding with it.

If you guide someone into trance, you are responsible for their physical safety and comfort till they have returned to ordinary consciousness. They will be less aware of dangers and also less aware of temperature extremes, fatigue, or other physical strains. Never leave a tranced person alone.

The relaxation techniques that we use are stress busters, useful in all areas of life. Our shared imagery is also useful in private meditation. Furthermore, repeated practice builds up the images in our minds, making subsequent exercises more vivid and more effective. So be sure to suggest and frequently repeat that people can use these techniques to visit these "places" as often as they need to or want to, and that doing so is a good thing. Always reinforce this suggestion before concluding a trance session.

Be sure that people have returned fully from trance to normal waking consciousness and have grounded fully. *The only way people might be harmed by inner work is through incomplete return, so take great care with this.* You might ask them to stand up and stretch, or to speak their own names out loud. Food and drink also help to complete reorientation. Be careful to draw full closure on the mentoring session before the student leaves. Talking about the trance experiences shortly after return, usually in the same session, helps fix them in memory. Encourage sharing, but do not force it. People should also pay particular attention to both day and night dreams for a few days after doing any trance work. Encourage people to keep journals that include their trance and dream experiences.

ROUGH SPOTS: POTENTIAL PROBLEMS
Too Little (Dark Night of the Soul)

Sometimes the path seems to be nothing but a treadmill.

Sometimes it just doesn't happen. Meditation is just boring. Ritual devolves into second-rate performance art. Nothing is moving or growing inside, and we fear that it was never anything but self-delusion. The cherished sense of Presence is absent.

This happens, periodically, to all of us. It's never easy. But it's hardest for beginners. Maybe they had that first surprising peak experience. They set out with great enthusiasm to find more of the same. For a while, all goes well, and then . . . the wave recedes, leaving them on the beach. They may feel abandoned, confused, disappointed — even cheated.

You know by the fact that you've had a few such dry spells of your own that your students will have them too.

In the literature of mysticism, this is known as the "dark night of the soul," the periods when Deity seems to withdraw, leaving the seeker alone and scared. If you think about it, there's some bleak comfort to be found in the very fact that the phenomenon is common enough to have been named.

The first thing to do for a student in the doldrums is to let them know that what they are suffering through is a normal part of the process and that they haven't failed in some way to make the cut.

Here are some further possibilities you may discuss with your student:

- They might be ill or run down. Suggest that they have a medical checkup. They should focus on their physical health. If possible, they might want to take a vacation. In any case, they should spend a couple of weeks on self-nurturance and get plenty of rest and play, eat healthily, exercise, etc.
- Some other current concerns might be claiming major energy or focus at this time. If there's a crisis at work or a family member is seriously ill, it's normal to be distracted. They may be worrying about paying bills. They may be at odds with a loved one. They may need to catch up with other responsibilities at home. Whatever it is, suggest that they take whatever time they need to resolve any stressors in their lives.

- The problem might be old hurts and unresolved issues from the past, even from early childhood. Working through this material can be difficult and painful, and may even require the assistance of a therapist. The things we would rather not know about ourselves can be personified as monsters or demons. Traditional occultists call them the *guardians at the gateway* and contemporary therapists call them the *shadow*. They obstruct our entrance to the inner realms and to the Otherworld. Before we can proceed, we must do something far more frightening than face them down — we must make peace with them.[9]

Any attempt to release this sort of blockage comes perilously close to therapy. Be very sure of your abilities before you try any active intervention. Suggest to your student that, when they feel grounded and brave, they make some symbolic gesture to indicate their willingness to listen. Maybe they could consecrate a conch shell, then listen to it meditatively for a few minutes daily. Be gentle and patient; this is not anything you want to force or rush at all.

Teach your student to ground and center. If frightening images start to come up in dream or meditation, advise them to make sure they are well grounded and centered and to stay with the images for as long as they can. Remember that the common cold seems worst just before it gets better, while it is "breaking up." They should record the images in their journal, try to find associations for them, and observe how they change over time.

- Finally, and most probably, they may simply be in a fallow period, comparable to an artist's periods of creative block. Everything new begins invisibly in the dark: seeds in the ground, babies in the womb, and deeds in the dream. Again, gentle patience is essential. You would not dig up a seed every day to see whether it is sprouting.

Some of the older writing about spirituality suggests that Deity intentionally withdraws for a while in order to force the seeker to send down deeper roots. This metaphor makes some sense to me because I've heard gardeners describe treating their vegetable patches in precisely that way.

Please notice that one unifying theme connects all four situations: being gentle and patient. And being good to oneself meanwhile. Remind your student (or yourself) to destress. Get plenty of rest. Eat healthy food. Exercise. Play and have fun. Not to force or rush anything, but keep up the basic daily meditation, if only for fifteen minutes a day, so as to notice when the cycle turns again. We wouldn't pave the garden just because there's a drought, now would we?

Too Much (Spiritual Emergency)

A *spiritual emergency* is a crisis that occurs when a person who is actively engaged in some meditative or spiritual practice becomes overwhelmed by the intensity of the experiences they achieve, which may be sudden, chaotic or dramatic, or reveal unpalatable truths. People may become frightened or confused and encounter problems in coping with normal responsibilities such as jobs and relationships. They may need some training and some time to assimilate what they have learned and rebalance their lives. Until this integration has happened, they may seem crazy indeed.

Mystics and lunatics can display some very similar behaviors, such as grandiosity (identification with Deity), delusions (visions and voices), hysterical symptoms (stigmata), or ritual behavior that appears to be obsessive or compulsive (hours of chanting or drumming).[10] A person who has not yet learned to navigate such altered states appropriately can be almost indistinguishable in action from somebody whose navigational systems are broken or missing. Their panic doesn't just look the same, it *is* the same. Someone — often some doctor — who doesn't understand that this particular apparent lunatic might really be a poet or mystic in the making cannot be blamed for perceiving them as sick, crazy, perhaps dangerously so. Mental illness really does exist, and really does great harm.

If a person in spiritual emergency enters the secular mental health system, their process is likely to be aborted by psychiatric drugs such as tranquilizers, which will force them back into the conventional mold. They will return to ordinary reality unchanged, neither a mystic nor a lunatic. This is certainly better than being permanently caught in lunacy and chaos. But those are not our only choices.

To prevent some of this sad misdiagnosis and mistreatment, transpersonal psychologists and their allies proposed a new diagnostic category, *Religious or Spiritual Problem*, which was incorporated into the fourth (and latest) edition of the *Diagnostic and Statistical Manual*.[11] DSM-IV, as it is called, is a diagnostic classification system used by all psychotherapists, establishing a common language that enables communication among mental health professionals. *Spiritual problems* are defined in DSM-IV as distressing experiences that involve a person's relationship with a transcendent being or force, but are not necessarily related to organized religion.[12]

People with spiritual problems need help, but not the same kind of help that mentally ill people need, despite some similarities of symptoms. The specific help they need can come from mentors who have learned what is needful from their own experiences on the same path into the Otherworld.

In plain English, spiritual emergency is more like "charley horse" pains, muscle cramps that we experience when we work out too much too soon, and less like sickness. The last thing you want when you get a charley horse is to become permanently sedentary. You back off on the activity, wait till the spasm passes, then start again more carefully. You may want to find yourself an experienced coach or trainer.

This more hopeful perception that the crisis can be resolved and transcended is also supported by anthropologists of religion who study the remaining intact Pagan and shamanic religious traditions of indigenous peoples. Additional supporting evidence comes from a new subdiscipline, the anthropology of consciousness.[13]

(When we emulate tribal peoples, cultural appropriation is a real concern, a complex and difficult issue. Still, for neo-Pagans, piecing together our own traditions from shards and shreds, the more continuous indigenous traditions [sadly, very few are pristine] are precious and indispensable models. We must always give proper credit, always support indigenous peoples' efforts to preserve and protect the integrity of their cultures as much as we can, and never claim to actually be part of any indigenous tradition unless we have fully entered that people's lifeways.)

Remember, shamanic threshold illness was one of the four possibilities for approaching altered states presented earlier in this chapter. On every continent where shamanic practice still exists, threshold illness, often called *crisis illness*, is a major and well-recognized entryway into the role of the shaman.[14] Particular symptoms are understood to announce a Sacred calling, identifying the person who can easily move between ordinary reality and the Otherworld, realm of dreams and visions. This is not a gentle or easy process. It's more like an abduction: shattering, chaotic, and painful, sometimes lasting for years. Yet there are things to be learned in that state about Otherworld travel and interactions with the beings and forces the shaman encounters while there.

> The crisis of a powerful illness can also be the central experience of the shaman's initiation. It involves an encounter with forces that decay and destroy. The shaman not only survives the ordeal of a debilitating sickness or accident, but is healed in the process. Illness thus becomes the vehicle for a higher plane of consciousness. The evolution from a state of psychic and physical disintegration to shamanizing is effected through the experience of self-cure. The shaman — and only the shaman — is a healer who has healed himself or herself; and as a healed healer, only he or she can truly know the territory of disease and death.[15]

> The future shaman sometimes takes the risk of being mistaken for a "madman" . . . but his "madness" fulfills a mystic function; it reveals certain aspects of reality to him that are inaccessible to other mortals, and it is only after having experienced and entered into these hidden dimensions of reality that the "madman" becomes a shaman.[16]

> A sickness that is understood as a process of purification, as the onset of enhanced psychic sensitivity giving access to the hidden and highest potentials of human existence, is therefore marked by very different characteristics than those ascribed to pathological conditions by modern medicine and psychology — namely that suffering has only negative consequences. According to the modern view, illness disrupts and endangers life, whereas the shaman

experiences his sickness as a call to destroy this life within himself so as to hear, see and live it more fully and completely in a higher state of awareness.[17]

Balanced between worlds, the shaman teaches by powerful example that illness can be a passageway to a greater life where there is access to great power at great risk.[18]

Understand, however, that this crisis, even when severe and long lasting, is only the first part of becoming a shaman. New shamans, initially identified and called by sickening crisis, then receive careful training from elders. They learn how to exercise voluntary control over their movement between states of consciousness. They learn when trance is or is not culturally appropriate. Most important, they learn to use their altered states in the service of their community. To become a shaman requires *both* talent and training.

Traditional cultures know that, just as some people are trapped in ordinary reality, others can be trapped in delusion. The shaman is the "technician of the Sacred," the one who moves with craft and care between the Worlds of Form and Spirit. Their presence in a community helps keep these worlds in lively contact.

So the person who is shattered by their introduction to the Otherworld is not necessarily forever broken in mind. More likely, they're in a state of spiritual emergency or shamanic crisis, two phrases describing much the same confused and over-whelmed mental state. They have newly opened gifts. They can learn how to use these gifts creatively, be dazzled into dysfunction by them, or seal them up again and hide them back in the base-ment. By giving people in crisis some safe space for experimenting, some caring instruction, some time and patience, we can help them become adept in the use of their gifts to the benefit of all.

A word right now to the solitary seeker: If you've run into any kind of difficulty, *find a support system before you proceed!* If you have not yet run into problems, find a support system anyhow. It's so much better to have a support system you don't need than to need one you don't have. How do you recognize psycho-spiritual danger? When your practice or its outcomes are interfering with your interpersonal relations, job, school performance, or physical health, problems are developing. An old spiritual song reminds us that "You have to walk that lonesome valley by yourself." Maybe so, but the wise take along a map and let somebody know their planned route and estimated time of return.

Another important caution: Sometimes mental or behavioral symptoms are caused by organic brain disease. The risk of using the medical model inappropriately is that we might force the person back into conventional ways. The antithetical risk is far worse: if the person's brain is physically damaged and they do not see a doctor, they may soon be dead of a brain hemorrhage or tumor.

It gets more complicated. Some disturbances arise from emotional trauma or from subtle chemical imbalances in the brain. There's an ongoing debate about which of these two is the most basic cause, and which is the effect that in turn causes behavioral symptoms. If trauma drives chemical change, then a spiritual breakthrough that is overwhelming enough to throw the person into crisis might produce very similar chemical effects.[19] In that case, analyzing their brain chemistry won't help us distinguish spiritual breakthrough from emotional breakdown.

Trauma itself is also a complicated subject. Some abuse memories are delusional, and some may even be cynically inserted, but trauma and intentional abuse also really happen to people. It's also possible that traumatic events can force a person past their habitual, conventional worldview, precipitating a genuine spiritual breakthrough. There are even instances where strong, skilled ritual interventions have helped people redefine and appropriate their traumatic experiences as initiations into the compassionate calling of the wounded healer.[20]

Even when the disturbances are clearly subsequent to intense spiritual practice, it's possible that by opening the inner world, the seeker has awakened painful memories that must be worked through before pursuing any deeper explorations.

If you are known in the community as a mentor, people in emergency will seek your aid. It may be one of your own students. More likely, it will be someone who has been experimenting on their own, without the support of a group or the guidance of a teacher. They may be reluctant — and with good reason — to turn to a secular therapist. They may know you socially, or know of your good reputation, and feel they can trust you to understand what they are going through.

So prepare yourself. Learn as much as you can about spiritual emergency before you need to know it. Someday, ready or not, somebody will phone or show up, in crisis, confused and scared. You may even hit some rocky stretches on your own personal path. No more time to learn or think — now you have to Do Something, hopefully something helpful. But what?

Here are three immediate goals, "first aid" for people in spiritual emergency: (1) help the person in crisis calm down, (2) help them learn some basic navigational skills, and (3) help them find some support systems, in both this world and the Other. I can also offer some specific recommendations:

- Make them physically comfortable. They may be thirsty, chilled or overheated, hungry, dirty and disheveled, sleep-deprived. Take care of those needs first — they're the easiest. Physical comfort is calming. More important, you are giving them immediate, tangible proof that you care.

- Help them ground. There may be specific methods that you've learned, or even some that are normal practices of your Tradition. Those your student is already familiar with will work best, of course. Beyond that, consider asking your student or friend to touch the Earth or hug a tree, take a salt bath, stretch, or eat some grounding food (hot broth or hot milk can work wonders).

- Suggest that they take whatever time they need — at least a month — to process and integrate the experiences that overwhelmed them before they engage in any additional Otherworld exploration.

  During this "time out," suggest that they avoid overstimulation as much as possible. No loud music, no crowds. They should stay away from situations in which they feel anxious or stressed. They might want to work around the house or garden; any physical activity is grounding. Consciously making their environment clean and orderly is a good focus for now, a metaphor for the inner task at hand. They should certainly get lots of sleep, eat a healthy and balanced diet, get enough rest and exercise, and try for a good belly laugh and a good orgasm every day.

- Create a *holding environment* when your friend feels ready to reexamine whatever upset them, a space that is protected and set apart, in which they can reflect upon what happened, perhaps figure out what it means, with your support and without risk of getting overwhelmed again. Your regular mentoring session will do if you're deliberate and formal about opening and closing the session.

  One of the most important things you can do for your student is to make sure that they know how to make psychic boundaries for their own private spiritual practice. These serve as a sort of vestibule between the worlds. It serves the same purpose for us that a well-maintained airlock does for an astronaut. Help your students find some way of clearly opening and closing each working session, to protect themselves from overwhelming flashbacks.

- *Listen.* Find out exactly what happened, on all planes. What methods did they use to enter the Otherworld? What did they see or hear while there? Don't interrupt or judge — just listen. Ask questions only for clarification. Probe very gently if at all. Back off at once if they begin to resist.

  Destressing is the first important step towards working through and integrating the experience. If they get agitated while explaining what took place, remind them to breathe slowly and deeply and to consciously relax their muscles. Also, make mental note of figures they met in the Otherworld, or things they saw or did, especially those that elicited a strong emotional reaction.

  While you listen, they are no longer facing whatever overwhelmed them alone. Your calm helps them calm down. Knowing that others, like you, have traveled the Otherworld and returned fully functional and bearing gifts lends them confidence.

- Let them cry or scream or even beat up on your couch if they need to. They need to release some of the pressure. Watch over their physical safety. Make sure nobody else in your house is being upset by the noise.

- Give them general information about shamanic crisis and spiritual emergency, so they can fit their experiences into a context in which these experiences, however strenuous, are not necessarily "sick."

- Help them understand the specific details of their own Otherworld experience in a historical and anthropological context. There are some remarkable similarities found in shamanic symbolism across cultures: the experience of flying or falling, the world-tree or vertical axis, challengers, wise advisers, animal spirits, dismemberment and rebirth. It will be useful for you and your student to do a bit of reading on what these symbols typically mean or represent.

Realizing that others have met the same figures, shared the same experiences, and thrived will add to your student or friend's confidence. Every time they find parallels for some image, their experience is further validated. They may also find more positive interpretations for the specific figures or activities that dismayed them. Dismemberment imagery, for example, may mean getting rid of useless burdens in preparation for great adventures.

Most confirming of all, if possible, is to help them discern the connections between their Otherworld experience and the lore of your own Tradition. These correspondences strengthen their connection to the people, symbols, and practices that nurtured their spiritual exploration up to this point.

• Also encourage them to explore their own personal meanings and associations to those symbols, using the same sorts of techniques that we use to work with our dreams. Keeping a journal of this discovery process is, as always, a good idea.

• Help them connect with experienced and supportive people. The wise Doctor Turtle advised me to send the lunatic to hang out with the poets. I recommend introducing your student to a couple of willing "buddies," people who have explored the Otherworld and successfully worked through their own emergence crisis, and who are willing to be there for your student or friend — not as authority figures, but as role models, peer-helpers, and understanding friends. It's particularly important for them to connect with people working within the same Tradition, especially group leaders or elders, who can help them apply traditional insights to their experience.

• Make sure they know how to ground and center themselves. I also strongly recommend that you work with them in trance to discover or create a personal safe space in the Otherworld. What this looks like exactly depends on the person. It might be the cool shade of a tree or a cushy chair by a warm, glowing hearth. Also, please help them connect with some wise Otherworldly allies and guides that can assist their explorations. (As I write this, the image of an astral collie dog walking at my side arises).

If they have trouble working through the first overwhelming experience, even with your help and support, it's time to seek a professionally trained therapist. They should also seek professional help if recovery from the first experience seemed to go well, but they got overwhelmed again when they resumed active practice. Your student or friend might have some emotional problems that need focused attention first. The Spiritual Emergence Network[21] may be able to help you find a local therapist who can work with both shamanic crisis and ordinary mental illness. Healing and growth are always possible.

When the initial spiritual emergency is resolved, and the person can travel safely, skillfully, and appropriately between the World of Form and the Otherworld, an obvious question arises: Why? For what purpose do some of us dare to seek the realm of the Gods?

I urge people to enter the Otherworld as a student, or even a diplomat — not as a tourist. This strenuous and perilous journey is no vacation from normal responsibilities. True bards and shamans journey in service to the people. They bring back wise answers to perplexities, new insights and inspiration, healing for lost or unbalanced souls. They maintain communication between humankind and Spirit. They sustain the group spirituality of each community they serve, nurturing our collective soul.

In general, as science is now beginning to admit, people benefit by opening themselves to Deity. It improves health and promotes healing. It gives us a sense of belonging, a centerpoint for our lives, which adds to our emotional stability. It provides, as all of human history shows us, an outlet for creative self-expression. It sustains us through the hard times that are part of every life. It gives us a channel for our devotion and our service.

By patient and consistent spiritual practice, we invite the awen, the power of the Entheoi, to flow and shine through all aspects of our lives.

It's worth the work; it's worth the risk.

TO LEARN MORE

**First, read the "Code of Ethics for Spiritual Guides,"
developed by the Council on Spiritual Practices and included,
by their gracious permission, as Appendix B in this book.**

BOOKS

Read these two first:

McColman, Carl. *The Aspiring Mystic.* Holbrook: Adams Media, 2000. ISBN 1580624162

This book is written for seekers rather than mentors. It is also permeated by Christian assumptions about theology and mysticism. It's still well worth reading and recommending to your students. McColman focuses on practice rather than theory. The book is accessible and full of gentle common sense.

Taylor, Kylea. *The Ethics of Caring*. Santa Cruz: Hanford Mead, 1995. ISBN 0964315815

   The Ethics of Caring is absolutely essential for Pagan mentors. It deals well with ethical concerns for anybody in any of the helping professions. What makes it particularly important for us is that it emphasizes the ethical issues involved in working with clients in altered states of consciousness.

Then read these, if you want greater depth:

Bragdon, Emma. *A Guidebook for Helping People in Spiritual Emergency*. Los Altos: Lightening Up Press, 1988. ISBN 0962096008

Cortright, Brant. *Psychotherapy and Spirit: Theory and Practice in Transpersonal Psychotherapy*. Albany: SUNY Press, 1997. ISBN 0791434664

Eliade, Mircea. *Shamanism: Archaic Techniques of Ecstasy*. 1964. Reprint, London: Arkana, 1989. ISBN 0691017794

Grof, Stanislav and Christina Grof, eds. *Spiritual Emergency: When Personal Transformation Becomes a Crisis*. Los Angeles: Tarcher, 1989. ISBN 0874775388

James, William. *The Varieties of Religious Experience*. 1902. Reprint, New York: Modern Library, 1994. ISBN 0679600752

   Originally published in 1902, this volume is full of assumptions derived from evangelical Protestantism.

Kalweit, Holger. *Dreamtime and Inner Space: The World of the Shaman*. Boston: Shambhala, 1984. ISBN 0877734062

Maslow, Abraham H. *Religions, Values and Peak-Experiences*. 1970. Reprint, New York: Penguin Arkana, 1994. ISBN 0140194878

Underhill, Evelyn. *Mysticism*. 1910. Reprint, Mineola: Dover Publications,

2002. ISBN 0486422380 (There is also a New American Library edition, published in 1974: ISBN 0452007844.)

Originally published in 1910, this volume is very dated and very biased, but is a classic in the field.

WEB SITES

<www.atpweb.org>: the Association for Transpersonal Psychology.
<www.blackboard.com>: a cyber learning site; includes David Lukoff's excellent and free course on spiritual emergency.
<www.ciis.edu/comserv/sen.html>: the Spiritual Emergence Network site, a referral source for therapists who understand spiritual emergence.
<www.internetguides.com/se/index.html>: the Spiritual Emergency Resource Center.
<www.shamanicdimensions.net>: resources on Shamanism.
<www.spiritmoving.com>: Selene Vega's site, with good resources on spiritual emergence.
<sunny.moorpark.cc.ca.us/~jbaker/sac/home.html>: the Society for the Anthropology of Consciousness.

NOTES

[1] William James, *The Varieties of Religious Experience* (New York: Collier, 1961), 165.

[2] Judy Harrow, *Wicca Covens* (Secaucus: Citadel, 1999), especially Chapter 7 (pp. 139–69) and Chapter 11 (pp. 244–58).

[3] This idea comes from Leon Reed, who has for many years been a respected Pagan teacher in Seattle.

[4] Abraham H. Maslow, *Religions, Values and Peak-Experiences* (1970; reprint, New York: Penguin Arkana, 1994), 60.

[5] Ibid., 59–68.

[6] Ibid., 22.

[7] This excerpt is from Bridger and Hergest's essay "Pagan Deism," originally published in *The Pomegranate* 1 (Feb. 1997): 37–42, and now available on the Proteus Coven Web site, <www.draknet.com/proteus/triangle.htm>.

[8] The Proteus Coven Web site contains much more detailed information about these techniques. See <www.draknet.com/proteus>.

[9] See Jeremiah Abrams and Connie Zweig, eds., *Meeting the Shadow* (Los Angeles: Tarcher, 1991).

[10] David Lukoff, "The Diagnosis of Mystical Experiences with Psychotic Features," *Journal of Transpersonal Psychology* 17.2. (1985): 155–81; Colleen Ward, *Altered States of Consciousness and Mental Health: A Cross-Cultural Perspective* (Newbury Park: Sage, 1989); and Ken Wilber, "The Pre/Trans Fallacy," *ReVision* 3.2 (1980): 51–72.

[11] *Diagnostic and Statistical Manual of Mental Disorders*, 4th ed. (Washington: American Psychiatric Association, 1994), 685.

[12] For some of the scholarly debate that preceded the adoption of this category, see *Dissociation* 4.4 (Dec. 1993) [theme issue on spirit possession] and *Transcultural Psychiatric Research Review* 29.4 (1992) [theme issue on spirit possession and trance].

[13] See <sunny.moorpark.cc.ca.us/~jbaker/sac/home.html>, the Web site of the Society for the Anthropology of Consciousness.

[14] Mircea Eliade, *Shamanism: Archaic Techniques of Ecstasy* (Princeton: Princeton University Press, 1964). See especially Chapter 2, "Initiatory Sicknesses and Dreams" (pp. 33–66).

[15] Joan Halifax, *Shamanic Voices* (New York: Dutton, 1979), 10–11.

[16] Mircea Eliade, *Myths, Dreams, and Mysteries* (New York: Harper & Row, 1960), 80–81.

[17] Holger Kalweit, *Dreamtime and Inner Space* (Boston: Shambhala, 1988), 91.

[18] Halifax, *Shamanic Voices*, 18.

[19] Based on readings from: *Scientific American: Mind and Brain* (New York: Freeman, 1993); Eugene d'Aquili and Andrew B. Newberg, *The Mystical Mind: Probing the Biology of Religious Experience* (Minneapolis: Fortress, 1999); Alexander L. Hinton, ed., *Biocultural Approaches to the Emotions* (Cambridge: Cambridge University Press, 1999); Daniel Kimble and Andrew M. Colman, eds., *Biological Aspects of Behavior* (London, Longman, 1995); Charles D. Laughlin et al., *Brain, Symbol and Experience: Toward a Neurobiology of Human Behavior* (Boston: Shambhala, 1990); Joseph LeDoux, *The Emotional Brain* (New York: Touchstone, 1998); and Joseph LeDoux and William Hirst, eds., *Mind and Brain: Dialogues in Cognitive Neuroscience* (Cambridge: Cambridge University Press, 1986).

[20] Based on readings from: David R. Johnson et al., "The Therapeutic Use of Ritual and Ceremony in the Treatment of Post-Traumatic Stress Disorder," *Journal of Traumatic Stress* 8.2 (1995): 283–98; Vanja Karth, "Using Ritual to Reclaim Young People in Trouble with the Law," <www.uct.ac.za/depts/criminology/articles/rites.htm>; Radha J. Parker and H. Shelton Horton, "A Typology of Ritual: Paradigms for Healing and Empowerment," *Counseling and Values* 40.2 (Jan. 1996): 82–97; Steven M. Silver and John P. Wilson, "Native American Healing and Purification

Rituals for War Stress," in *Human Adaptation to Extreme Stress*, ed. John P. Wilson et al. (New York: Plenum, 1988); Richard A. Whiting, "Guidelines to Designing Therapeutic Rituals," in *Rituals in Families and Family Therapy*, ed. Evan Imber-Black et al. (New York: Norton, 1988); John P. Wilson, ed., "Culture and Trauma: The Sacred Pipe Revisited," in *Trauma, Transformation and Healing* (New York: Brunner-Mazel, 1989); and Susan M. Winslow, "The Use of Ritual in Incest Healing," *Smith College Studies in Social Work* 61.1 (Nov. 1990): 27–41.

For much more, visit the Web site of the National Center for Post-Traumatic Stress Disorder, <www.ncptsd.org> and search their "PILOTS" database using the keywords *ritual therapy*.

[21] See <www.ciis.edu/comserv/sen.html>, the Web site of the Spiritual Emergence Network.

Community

CHAPTER 6

SHARING SUPPORT

TO HAVE A CONVERSION EXPERIENCE IS NOTHING much. The real thing is to be able to keep on taking it seriously; to retain a sense of its plausibility. This is where the religious community comes in.[1]

We are all longing to go home to some place we have never been — a place half-remembered and half-envisioned we can only catch glimpses of from time to time. Community. Somewhere, there are people to whom we can speak with passion without having the words catch in our throats. Somewhere a circle of hands will open to receive us, eyes will light up as we enter, voices will celebrate with us whenever we come into our own power. Community means strength that joins with our strength to do the work that needs to be done. Arms to hold us when we falter. A circle of healing. A circle of friends. Someplace where we can be free.[2]

Among ourselves, we don't even call it *conversion*, we call it *homecoming*. We discover that there is a name for religious feelings we had all along, and that there are others who feel as we do. We realize that we are no longer alone. We take root and grow.

Community means the whole web of human relationships that support and nurture us: large and small, intimate and extended, formal and informal; all the ways in which we connect with people of like mind and common interest. Here, we are specifically discussing religious community, the human context for each person's spiritual development. Community is what makes spirituality sustainable. The Pagan community, like other religious communities, validates, nurtures, instructs, supports, and challenges each member. It's not perfect, but it's good enough — and it's certainly much better than isolation.

Community cannot exist without trust, and the strongest basis for trust is shared ethics. We need to know what we can expect from one another.

ETHICS: FINDING GUIDANCE

Philosophers have been talking about ethics for as long as philosophers have been talking about anything. The history and development of ethical theories is a fascinating subject, but not the one at hand. Our topic is adult spiritual development, and how to facilitate it.

I believe that the single most important religious question is, "How do I go about living by this?" How do I truly live by these values, by these insights? How do I act in accordance with the guidance and inspiration I receive from the Entheoi? How do I most clearly manifest the awen in my daily life? Ethics develop as people in community work together to answer these and related questions. Community creates ethics; ethics sustain community. Both anchor and support spirituality.

Kohlberg: Fairness and Rights

Lawrence Kohlberg (1927–1987) was confronted with a serious ethical dilemma as a young man, and felt he had little to guide him. As a result, understanding the reasoning behind people's ethics became his life's quest. He went back to college, eventually earned a doctorate in psychology, became a professor at Harvard, and devoted his career to studying ethical development. His work drew on the developmental stage theory of Erik Erikson and became one of James Fowler's main sources. Here's how the three link up:

ERIKSON	KOHLBERG	FOWLER
adolescent	conventional/conformist following the crowd	synthetic-conventional
early adulthood	conventional/ law and order following the rules	individuative-reflective
mature adulthood	conscientious following one's own conscience	conjunctive

And here are some of the defining characteristics for each of Kohlberg's three stages of ethical development:

PERSPECTIVE	AUTHORITY	MOTIVATION
peer group or immediate family	positional (if worthy)	conformity, avoiding shame
ethnic group or subculture	ideological	rules, fairness, pride
humanity as a whole (for Pagans, the whole Earth)	experiential, empathetic, infomed by cumulative wisdom	situational, care

Kohlberg's research, like Fowler's, consisted of structured interviews. His sample included teenagers and adults in the United States, Israel, and Turkey, three countries with three different religious cultures. Participants were presented with several ethical dilemmas. Probably the best known, the Heinz scenario, asked whether a man should steal medication to save his sick wife's life. Respondents' answers were rated more for the reasons they cited than for the actual choices they made, and common themes were identified. Kohlberg built his theories from these themes.

Like Erikson and Fowler, Kohlberg identified childhood stages and advanced stages that are only achieved by saints. Since most of our students are neither children nor saints, let's look more closely at the three realistic adult stages:

1. *Conventional/Conformist*. People at this stage very much want to fit in with some chosen group, and with the group's ways of doing things. They don't want to be embarrassed or shamed before the others. Following fads and fashions is harmless enough, but some pathological groups enforce a far more dangerous conformity — consider gangs or authoritarian and extremist religious groups. Authority is vested in the group's leaders as long as these individuals seem to be worthy of their position. The risk of this stage is groupthink, a failure to develop independent critical thought.

2. *Conventional/Law Abiding*. At this stage, people value social order and adherence to the rules. They tend to identify with a nationality or other such large group. Authority is vested in the guiding ideals of that group. Members follow the rules and avoid questioning basic premises. For a young adult just getting established in an occupation, it's important to be perceived as a team player. The same may apply to a new Pagan, seeking a place within our community. Patriotism is characteristic of this stage, or even bigotry, the invidious belief that our way is the one right way for everybody. The risk is that what is simply different may be perceived as wrong or threatening; that insularity can lead to conflict.

3. *Conscientious*. Kohlberg called this level *postconventional*. In this stage, the individual is guided by personal conscience and by abstract general moral principles. These principles are formed by the interaction of personal experience with the cumulative wisdom of that person's religion and/or culture. Customs and laws are important guidelines, but they are not infallible. People at this level may intentionally break laws and accept the consequences in the service of a greater good, as with conscientious objectors to war (or with those who plotted to assassinate Hitler). At the conscientious level, final authority resides within, with the still, small voices of the Entheoi. Ethical decisions are based on the situation at hand and are motivated by care. The risk of this level is self-delusion, the confusion of personal opinion with The Truth.

Please notice that these three stages move towards autonomy. The first features group conformity. The second emphasizes obedience to the laws. The third advances to situational decision making. Kohlberg's ethic is the ethic of fairness and freedom, an important part of growing up. But autonomy, in unbalanced extreme, turns to alienation. A "pure" abstract ethic places principle over people. Enter Carol Gilligan.

Gilligan: Relationship and Care

Carol Gilligan was a student of Kohlberg's at Harvard and worked with him as a research assistant. She noticed that all the subjects of his central research study were male. Since girls are raised and socialized very differently from boys, Gilligan set out to discover the differences in their ethical development. They were just what she expected to find:

. . . the very traits that traditionally have defined the "goodness" of women, their care for and sensitivity to the needs of others, are those that mark them (on Kohlberg's scale) as deficient in moral development. . . . When one begins with the study of women and derives developmental concepts from their lives, the outline of a moral conception different from that described by Freud, Piaget, or Kohlberg begins to emerge. . . . In this conception, the moral problem arises from conflicting responsibilities rather than from competing rights and requires for its resolution a mode of thinking that is contextual and narrative rather than formal and abstract. This conception of morality as concerned with the activity of care centers moral development around the understanding of responsibilities and relationships, just as the conception of morality as fairness ties moral development to the understanding of rights and rules. . . .

. . . the morality of rights differs from the morality of responsibility in its emphasis on separation rather than connection, in its consideration of the individual rather than the relationship as primary . . . [3]

For the most part, in our culture, young girls are raised with an ethic of care and affiliation. Young boys are raised with an ethic of fairness and rights. Carried to extreme, either results in pathological imbalance. Men can become coldly rule-bound, emotionally retarded, and incapable of intimate bonding. Women can become spineless and powerless, devoid of all self-assertion or initiative, limited to enabler roles. This is the gender role stereotyping that was still prevalent in the middle of the twentieth century and which we can even find reflected in some of the older neo-Pagan materials.

Fortunately, Gilligan found that as people come to full maturity, many also move towards balance:

> The morality of rights is predicated on equality and centered on the understanding of fairness, while the ethic of responsibility relies on the concept of equity, the recognition of differences in need. While the ethic of rights is a manifestation of equal respect, balancing the claims of other and self, the ethic of responsibility rests on an understanding that gives rise to compassion and care. Thus the counterpoint of identity and intimacy . . . is articulated through two different moralities whose complementarity is the discovery of maturity . . . both integrity and care must be included in a morality that can encompass the dilemmas of love and work that arise in adult life.[4]

Pagan Polarity

Let me emphasize Gilligan's findings: Ethical maturity consists of the complementary and dynamic balance of freedom and responsibility, of autonomy and affiliation. This is another of those both/and situations, where Pagans refuse to choose between two good things. And have we a more concise, simple, and familiar way to express this essential balance? We surely do:

> *An it harm none, do what you will.*

The first phrase expresses the ethic of care, the second the ethic of rights.

The Rede is a core ethic, a central guiding principle, a very general statement. Like any other community, we have some specific mutual understandings, rules, and customs that apply this principle to our shared religious activity and to our secular lives.

Pagans have very few, for we pride ourselves on our "high choice" ethic, but we hold them dearly. Here are mine:

- *Respect for privacy.* I don't reveal information given to me in confidence. I don't reveal the identities of other Pagans without their express permission. Unless we can trust each other with this, there can be no community.
- *Respect for autonomy.* I don't force my will on others. Neither do I allow others to force their will on me. I do not actively intervene in another person's life without their express permission.
- *Respect for nature.* As much as an urban dweller can, I live by a conservation ethic. I try not to waste. I recycle whenever possible. I support environmental causes.
- *Personal responsibility.* Although I know that I was formed by all my past experiences, some of which were completely beyond my control, I take responsibility for the life I create from this day forward. Although I know that events and forces completely beyond my control will affect me in the future, I take responsibility for how I act in any circumstances.
- *Congruence.* I will do my best to live in accordance with my values. I expect and hope to be judged more by my deeds than by my words.

Values

Mentors may be asked to help our students discern their own core values and make complex ethical choices.

Value is derived from the Latin *valere*, which means strong or worthy. Two closely related words from the same Latin root are *valor* and *valid*. Our values are those things, activities, or qualities that are strong and worthy, high priorities in our lives. What the psychologists call *values*, occultists would more typically call *true will*. Nothing new to us so far, except language.

What the psychologists and educators can add is the concept of *values clarification*, a process by which people can become aware of their core values. Consciousness opens up our choices, both about our values and our actions, so that we can harmonize them better. When a person's values and behavior become congruent, a great deal of personal energy is freed up.

Here are the key points I think we can learn from humanistic psychology:

- Unlike our minimalist ethics, personal values are prescriptive. They tell us what we should do, not just what to avoid. Therefore they must be freely chosen. Living from personal values is both a far freer and far more demanding lifestyle than blind obedience.
- Because values guide our personal priorities within the World of Form, they must be chosen from among alternatives and within realistic limits.
- Values are manifested by attitudes and actions, not mere statements. People who are growing will manifest their values by increasingly congruent attitudes and actions.

(By now it's easy to see why fundamentalists of all religions are so bitterly opposed to education about values clarification: those who believe there is only one right way are horrified by the possibility and responsibility of choice. In their view, children are property or puppets, to be programmed with their parents' values.)

Communities and cultures have identifiable collective values. A person's individual values (e.g., to be a doctor or a dancer) are usually specific applications of their community's general values (e.g., self-actualization). When, at the conscientious level, personal and community values conflict, tragic choices ensue. Thankfully, this is rare.

But I can find no universal values and no universally applicable standards for determining which values are "good" or "bad." Self-actualization is not prized in all cultures. Some value the family and community far above the individual, to the point of believing that "the nail that sticks up must be hammered down." Also notice my pejorative reference to "blind obedience" a few paragraphs ago. Some of our neighbors perceive poverty, obedience, and chastity as particularly holy virtues. Pagans certainly don't. Perhaps values are just a matter of taste, of esthetics.

If this is so, then there is clearly no basis for a community to impose any specific prescriptive values on its members. As long as we do no harm, what we do is nobody's business but our own. On the other hand, it makes sense for people concerned with their own growth to choose a community of like-minded folk, where they will find a supportive context for their efforts to discern their own core values and live in accordance with those. Then what we do becomes other people's business, because we choose to make it so.

We are this kind of voluntary community, a first-generation religion still mostly made up of converts, people who consciously chose this path. It becomes far more complicated in successive generations, but that discussion is tangential right now.

If communities, subcultures, and cultures are groups of people who hold certain values in common, then it's logical that there would be ways for such groups — both religious and secular — to work together to clarify and perhaps modify their collective values, as well as supporting individual members' growth.

Here are a few exercises for values clarification, which I derived from secular psychology and adapted for Pagan use.

VALUES CLARIFICATION EXERCISES

As usual, do these steps yourself before assigning them to a student.

1. Select a Goddess or God you've been feeling particularly attracted to, perhaps the one used for the immersion exercise in Chapter 5.

   Look up some good, poetic translations of materials from that Deity's original culture for myths, odes, and invocations concerning that Deity. Identify the values that are depicted in the stories and poems.

   Now do the same with some popular modern retellings. Are the values depicted there the same? If they are different, list the differences.

2. Identify any values that do not seem strong and worthy and try to figure out why. Then rank the ones that remain in the order of how intensely you feel them. Identify ways you have acted in accordance with those values within the past month.

3. Consider dropping any values you have not practiced recently from the list. For the top half of the remaining list, plan three ways to put them into practice within the next month.

4. Think about what you would put on a t-shirt (or in a signature file for email), a short phrase that describes you as you are right now, that you would want the world at large to see. What would it be?

5. Select three achievements so far that you would want to have written on your tombstone. These describe

your most significant and lasting contributions. Is there something you would like to have there that is not yet so? Plan three ways you can begin working towards that goal in the next month, and in the next year.

Customs

We also have a myriad of customs that have no real moral implications, but are still absolutely necessary for us to work together. A secular example might be driving on the right side of the street. In Europe, they drive on the left. Neither is more right or wrong than the other, but everybody who drives in a region needs to do the same, or some of them will die.

A person who is new to Paganism may not know these necessary conventions. Elders can help them learn. You know better than I what these are in your local area, along with the little turns of speech or fads of dress that do nothing at all except help us recognize one another.

New Pagans will almost certainly also need help understanding our variegated community and placing themselves within it.

NAVIGATING COMMUNITY

One thing we are not, thank the Gods, is a random collection of isolated individuals. All *healthy* human life is lived within a complex matrix of relationships.

Community is the very opposite of mass or mob. It is anything but a featureless aggregate of interchangeable parts. True community, like all other living things, has a complex and well-articulated internal structure. It consists of households, congregations, ball teams, block associations, choruses, unions, self-help groups — all those many settings where people gather around common concerns, needs, or interests. We can only truly know each other, share our lives, a very few at a time. It's so easy to get lost in a crowd.

This is important for everybody, but essential for spiritual seekers. We need support, need reality checks, because spiritual growth can be confusing, chaotic, risky. The Pagan community offers us many different ways to connect.

Working Partnerships

In some of the older, structured Traditions, it's customary for people to work in couples. Even when this is not the expected pattern, it's a very good idea. These pairings are called working partnerships, a cold term for so intimate a relationship. Working partners are playmates, workmates, and soul mates; best friends, confidants, and mutual mentors.[5] Partnerships cannot be assigned or forced. They can only grow naturally from mutual affinity. If you are mentoring people in partnerships, you may be asked to help resolve any conflicts they develop around their spiritual work.

Groups

Most of us prefer to worship and study in small, intimate groups: Witches' covens, Druid groves, etc. For very much more information about small Pagan groups, please see my earlier book, *Wicca Covens*.[6] Most mentors are group leaders. They prepare students for group membership and for advanced levels within the group.

Working within a group has many advantages. In group discussion, each member will bring up questions or comments that others had not thought of. Members encourage each other through difficult periods. Most important, the only way to learn teamwork is as part of a team.

There are other ways of teaching and learning. Some areas have open classes covering the basics. Students who do well in one of these classes may be referred to a group or a personal teacher. Sometimes a student can't join a group because they live too far away, their schedules conflict, or they don't get along well with somebody already in that group. The group leader may be willing to teach the student individually, as an "extern." And there are some solitary elders who mentor students individually.

If these alternatives are not available in your area, you might want to see about creating them, or others. Group work is not for everybody.

Traditions

The term *Tradition*, when capitalized, refers to one of the many inner orders of Paganism, particularly the Wiccan subgroup. If Pagan spirituality is a cluster of intertwining paths, each Tradition can be considered one path in the cluster. Some are closer than others. Some even run together for a stretch. But each has its own focal Deities, level of formality, organizational forms, etc. A mentor's job is to help the student find the Tradition where they fit in best. Even within the same Tradition, the person may fit more comfortably in some other group than yours. Sometimes the best service you can give a seeker is an appropriate introduction.

Traditions are passed from teacher to student, as Bell described so beautifully in Chapter 2. Eventually, students become teachers. We call this family-like process of transmission *lineage*. When we learn from each other directly, by working closely together and even by sharing transformative, initiatory experiences, we form intimate bonds, psychic links. Because all members of a particular lineage or Tradition are so linked, even if indirectly, we develop a kind of group mind, our own familial nexus in the collective unconscious. This we call an *egregore*.

Groups that work closely together over years have smaller, but more concentrated egregores, while the egregores of lineages are larger, but more diffuse. Like ingredients in a soup, each new person changes the overall "flavor" of an egregore and the smaller the group, the more noticeable the change.

Study can make a person learned. Individual practice can certainly open connection to the Ancient Gods. But a seeker can only be brought into an egregore by a person who is already a member, and who is empowered to do so. If you are a teaching elder within a Tradition, you are probably also one of the gate-keepers of that Tradition's egregore. Be careful, even prayerful, as you exercise this sacred privilege.

Organizations

There are several legally incorporated and recognized Pagan churches, established so that members can have the privileges and benefits of other clergy. Covenant of the Goddess,[7] now over a quarter century old, is limited to Witches, but parallel organiza-tions exist for other types of Pagans. Many of these groups organize advanced and continuing education programs. They also engage in interfaith outreach and public education, hoping to dispel the old stereotypes and help our neighbors understand us better. If your student has any interest in serving as public clergy, they will need to be affiliated with an organization that provides legal credentials. If they encounter any form of discrim-ination or harassment, these groups may be able to help.

I want to highlight the Military Pagan Network, an invaluable source of support for Pagans who have been separated from their home communities.[8] Kudos to them!

Ancillary Networks

Pagans use the Internet extensively, maintaining thousands of Web sites and discussion lists that help us share information and keep in touch.[9] There are also many small amateur magazines and some that are more professionally produced. Many yearly gatherings and festivals, both regional and national, give us the opportunity to meet one another, worship together, and share information through formal workshops and many informal conversations.[10] And, of course, there are informal networks, and even coven leaders' peer support groups in some localities. Mentors help students find appropriate resources.

What we don't have, and don't want, is a unitary, pyramidal structure that centralizes authority and fosters dependency. What we don't have, and don't want, is a religious bureaucracy that would divert our financial and human resources to its own self-perpetuation — we are not slaves to a building fund. What we don't have, and most certainly don't want, is anyone presuming to intervene or mediate between us and the Ancient Gods.

GIVING AND RECEIVING

One of the most important things we get from community is the opportunity to give. Grown-ups need that.

Many different theories of maturity have noticed and described the same need in different words. This convergence demonstrates that the need they are all describing is very real, very widespread.

Here are several different ways of saying the same thing: Mature adults need an outlet for creative self-expression. We need a sense of personal generativity. We need to feel that we are making a positive difference in our world, that we matter in some way. We need the self-esteem that derives from doing good work. We need to feel appreciated by others.

In spiritual terms, we need to keep the current moving. The awen we receive needs to flow through us into creative art and/or compassionate service, or it becomes blocked and stagnant and might break out in disruptive ways.

Buddhists have a series of pictures illustrating their religion's concept of sequential spiritual development, called the *ox herding pictures.* The surprise is that the one representing enlightenment is only next to last in the set. The final picture is called "returning to the village with helping hands."[11] In the religious culture most associated with meditation, we find the same insight that Sacred connection necessarily leads to human service.

I believe that our talents, which are gifts from the Gods, are also our callings. Developing those talents is our gift to the Gods and to Their people.

Community life is an intrinsic part of a Pagan spiritual path. In community, in service, we grow to be ourselves. Pagan mentors actively facilitate our students' mutually beneficial connections with our community in two related but different ways: through coaching and sponsoring.

Both of these approaches exist in the secular world — in sports, academia, the arts and professions, and business. Neither is about healing or fixing anything. Both are future-oriented and goal-directed, in the service of self-actualization.

Coaching

A coach, in the original meaning, is a person who trains or tutors others in specific skills, like a football coach or a drama coach. The coach might work with a team or might be a personal trainer, helping a trainee work towards a clearly defined goal, such as winning a marathon. Coaching is not normally directed towards generic self-improvement — it's about winning.

In the last twenty years or so, a new "coaching profession" has emerged. Most of these coaches were originally trained as counselors. They disliked the growing emphasis on managed care and the imposition of the medical model on counseling. Moving over to coaching was their way to resume working with clients towards development rather than remediation.

Much of this new coaching profession is career-oriented. Because of this, much of it is applicable for a student trying to discover how best to serve the community.

Here are some of the ways a Pagan mentor might coach a student:

- Hold a vision of who the student can be or become, the roles they might fulfill in our community. Demonstrate and communicate a belief in the student's potential, even when the student is feeling discouraged.
- Help the student define goals and outline strategies for reaching those goals.
- Help the student identify opportunities, what the community needs, what contributions would be most appreciated at this time.
- Help the student inventory their own talents, strengths, skills, and needs.
- Help the student make decisions about their role in the community or other areas of life, in accord with their core values and the leadings of the Entheoi, as well as more practical considerations.
- Encourage the student to act in accordance with these decisions.
- Sustain the process through periodic check-ins. Help the student evaluate results, reconsider goals if necessary, and plan next steps.
- Celebrate successes as they come.

Please notice that all this takes place strictly between mentor and student. Nobody else in the community needs to know that a coaching relationship exists. Similarly, in secular coaching, clients can have regular meetings with their coaches away from the workplace, even over the telephone. The coach does not need to interact with the client's supervisors or professional colleagues in any way.

Sponsoring

A coach can function well within an organization, perhaps as part of a Human Resources department, or completely outside it, in private practice. But a sponsor must be a respected part of the corporation, university, or agency in order to be effective.

A sponsor assumes responsibility for another person or a group during a period of instruction, apprenticeship, or probation. A sponsor vouches for a new person — or one who is simply more junior — until that person has had time to develop a good reputation of their own. A sponsor risks their own reputation by recommending people who have not yet proved themselves, so that both the newcomer and the community may survive and thrive. Every healthy community needs a younger generation of leaders, preparing to move the agenda.

You can hire a career coach and pay them by the session, just as you can hire a marriage counselor or a fitness trainer. There's nothing wrong with that, in secular life. But, even in the business world, nobody can righteously hire a sponsor. A purchased vouch is a worthless vouch, anywhere, anytime.

Important as vouching is, sponsors also do a great deal more. A Pagan sponsor

- introduces the newcomer to other elders;
- helps the newcomer assimilate rules and customs of our subculture;
- discusses ideas, challenges the newcomer's thinking;
- loans or recommends reading material; suggests classes or

lectures, exercises, etc.; generally lets newcomer know about resources in local area;

- gives feedback on work done, including suggestions for improvement;
- sets tasks for the newcomer that will either be learning experiences, high-visibility showcases, or both; and
- nominates the newcomer for high-visibility functions, brings them in to committee projects where other elders will observe their capabilities.

If we think of a coach as pushing a newcomer along, we might say that a sponsor pulls them inside.

We don't call it conversion when somebody comes to us — we call it homecoming. To extend the metaphor, mentors drive the Welcome Wagon, help the newcomers learn their way around the neighborhood, and learn the local ordinances and customs.

TO LEARN MORE

Wood, Robin. *When, Why . . . If*. Dearborn: Livingtree, 1996. ISBN 096529840x

    This book is an introduction to Pagan ethics and is as invaluable for seekers as Kylea Taylor's book, recommended in the previous chapter, is for mentors.

NOTES

  [1] Peter L. Berger and Thomas Luckmann, *The Social Construction of Reality* (New York: Doubleday, 1966), 158.
  [2] Starhawk, *Dreaming the Dark* (Boston: Beacon, 1982), 92.

3 Carol Gilligan, *In a Different Voice* (Cambridge: Harvard University Press, 1982), 18–19.

4 Ibid., 164–65.

5 See Judy Harrow, *Wicca Covens* (Secaucus: Citadel, 1999). Chapter 10 (pp. 210–53) is about working partnership. See also Alan Richardson, *Dancers to the Gods* (Wellingborough: Aquarian, 1985). This book describes the magical partnership of Christine Hartley and Charles Seymour circa the 1930s. Seymour was one of the earliest advocates for reviving Goddess worship.

6 See note 5 for publication information.

7 See <www.cog.org>.

8 See <www.milpagan.org>.

9 See M. Macha NightMare, *Witchcraft and the Web: Weaving Pagan Traditions On-Line* (Toronto: ECW Press, 2001) or visit The Witches' Voice Web site, <www.witchvox.com/>.

10 See Sarah Pike, *Earthly Bodies, Magical Selves* (Berkeley: University of California Press, 2001) for an in-depth study of festivals and gatherings.

11 See Willard Johnson, *Riding the Ox Home* (Boston: Beacon, 1987).

Lore

CHAPTER 7

SHARING KNOWLEDGE

THIS CHAPTER IS ABOUT TIME TRAVEL, SOMETHING humans have always been able to do. Our ancestors lived through a variety of experiences, some of them very different than our own. They learned from their experiences, just as we do from ours. They talked to each other, pooled their learning, and passed it to their children as lore. The next generation started with a certain knowledge base, to which they added. Eventually, we inherited this cumulative knowledge base.

We are the caretakers now. We correct, refine, extend what we have received, and then pass it all on to the next generation. All living traditions must change as circumstances change and as people learn. We live in a different time. We have different experiences and different, much better, tools. But our duty to keep the knowledge base healthy and growing remains precisely the same.

This heritage of lore allows us to consult our ancestors and teach our descendants. Without it, each generation would need to start from scratch as hunters and gatherers and cave-dwellers. Lore is what makes us human.

Miriam Benson, an elder of Proteus, writes:

I've told my daughter that humans have three great Magics: speaking, measuring, and writing.
- Speaking allows humans to teleport. Through description, we are present at another's event.
- Measuring gives us the ability to create and re-create environments.

- Writing gives us dimensional/time travel. Not only can
  we be present at events of those we never met, we can be
  a party to things that never happened, nor will happen.
  This encourages her not only to seek out that which is and
  try it on for size, but also to roll her own.[1]

Of course, lore came centuries before writing. The griot, the
shanachie, and the bard all transmitted lore orally. Culture existed
long before literacy. But writing made it much easier. The printing
press made it easier still. Today we have the Internet, by which we
transmit knowledge worldwide in a matter of minutes. These
tools that enable us to share lore also *are* lore, the result of
centuries of carefully accumulated knowledge.

As society became more complex and people began to specialize,
bodies of occupational lore developed. Bakers know things that
carpenters don't. From the perspective of only a century ago,
computer programmers practice the most arcane of magics. There
is a body of lore concerned with spirituality and religion. In fact, as
there are many religions in this world, many ways to approach
the Great Mystery, there are many bodies of religious lore.

Another of your major tasks as a Pagan spiritual mentor is to
introduce your students to Pagan religious lore, and to the lore of
your particular Tradition within the Pagan religious cluster. You
may also be introducing your students to the ancestors themselves
in a more direct way, in the Otherworld where their spirits dwell.
Let's start with that, for the ancestors created the lore.

ANCESTORS

I came to this religion as an adult, by choice rather than by family
tradition. To the best of my knowledge, I have not had a Pagan
ancestor for at least a thousand years. So although I knew that
many Pagan groups honor the ancestors, I was loath to participate

in this good custom. I feared that my own direct ancestors would disapprove of the religious choice I had made, and might even be offended if I called their names in a Pagan ritual.

All of us have genetic ancestors. I came to understand that we also have intellectual and spiritual ancestors, and that these are not necessarily the same people. So first let's take a moment to thank the spirits of all the nonrelatives who nurtured our child-selves: the schoolteachers, scout leaders, kindly neighbors, and parents of our friends. Just as they gave us some things our own parents could not, so we receive from historical figures some things we cannot derive from the dead of our own families.

ANCESTORS OF THE SPIRIT

Take the time to complete this exercise first, before recommending it to a student.

1. Take a plain, unlined sheet of paper. Write your name towards the top.
2. Identify people that have been a strong influence on you, leaving out family members and your direct mentors or teachers. These could be people whose writing has shaped your thinking (for me: George Orwell, Carl Rogers) or historical figures whose actions inspire you (for me: Emperor Julian the Faithkeeper, Thomas Morton of Merry Mount). You can include anybody who is important to you for any reason at all.
3. Now, add any genetic ancestors who actually influenced you. Be careful about this; my grandparents profoundly changed my life by immigrating here from Eastern Europe. Still, I know nothing at all about their spiritual or intellectual lives, and was not influenced by them. Accordingly, I would not place them on this chart.

4. Draw lines like roots down from your name. Make these lines thicker or thinner according to the importance of the influence, longer or shorter according to its closeness. Write one person's name at the end of each "root."

5. As much as you know, identify the people who influenced the ones who influenced you. Draw the branching roots in the same way you drew your own. Keep going till you run out of information. What you have will resemble a family tree.

6. With a different color pen, make brief notes about the nature of the influence: book titles, great deeds, qualities you would like to emulate, etc.

7. This is your intellectual and spiritual ancestry, your own personal "Mighty Dead." If you can't trace the influences back more than one or two "generations," you might want to research the earlier influences, to discover you own personal intellectual and spiritual roots. This is the inner plane parallel to genealogical research.

8. Another worthwhile exercise is to identify how each person recombined, modified, and augmented what they received from their own influences before passing it on to others.

The Mighty Dead

Among Pagans, I often heard the phrase *Mighty Dead*, but no definition or explanation was forthcoming. So I was left to define it for myself. What I worked out is entirely personal, not anything that carries the weight of tradition.

To me, *Mighty Dead* means something very similar to what my Catholic friends refer to as *saints*. That is, people who lived before us and whose stories we find instructive or inspirational; dead people who continue to guide us, at least by example and perhaps also by inner communication; dead people whose examples show us how to come closer to the Entheoi.

Catholics pray to saints whenever they please, but also dedicate a festival to their honor, called All Saints Day. By no coincidence at all, that is the same day as the Pagan feast of Samhain. We welcome our Mighty Dead at Samhain, but I know of no rule against honoring or even invoking them at any other time.

I don't usually speculate a lot about what happens to us after we die, since there's no way to test any of the theories people have created. Many Pagans believe in reincarnation. But reincarnated souls can't also be present in the Otherworld, available to respond to our invocations. Might it be that the worthy dead have a choice?

We've all heard stories about near-death experiences, some of which involve people choosing to return to a damaged body, possibly to lifelong pain or impairment, because they feel their children still need them. Perhaps others choose to reincarnate, so they can be with their descendants or other loved ones, offering more practical help to a more limited number. Spirits can't kiss a boo-boo to make it better. This choice might appeal to the ones who were more private and family-oriented in life.

Others, perhaps those who were more public and community-oriented, might choose to stay in the vestibules of the Otherworld, where they can communicate more freely with the living. These would be the saints, or the Mighty Dead, on whom we can call for assistance and guidance.

Buddhism offers an interestingly different perspective. Rebirth gives us all the chances we need to work towards enlightenment. Once we achieve it, we can go on to Nirvana, to perfect peace and bliss. But in the Buddhist model, some souls choose instead to become *bodhisattvas*, taking a compassionate oath to remain available as guides and teachers until all souls have become enlightened. They serve the same function as Catholic saints or Pagan Mighty Dead.

Catholics, of course, have an elaborate institutional procedure for determining just who is a saint. We don't. No problem. Each of us honors, and calls on, those people whose stories and legacies are strong and worthy for us. If they respond, they are clearly our Mighty Dead.

It's even possible that the dead remain nearby as long as they are remembered and needed, then go on to Nirvana, or to another incarnation, once living memory has faded. Again, memory will last longer for those who were public figures or who produced lasting works of scholarship or art than for a quiet, wise, loving grandparent who lived in relative obscurity.

So what actually happens when we invoke the Mighty Dead and feel a response? As far as I can tell the whole idea of direct communication with the dead is entirely speculative, if very satisfying. I could have built an image in my own deep mind based on memories of those I actually knew, or could have researched and studied historical figures — sort of an internal "expert system." Or we could have built a collective "expert system" that becomes part of our group's egregore. Perhaps I'm contacting a construct rather than a consciousness. Again, how would I tell the difference? Is there a reliable Turing test in the realm of spirit? If so, I've never heard of it.

Some people are disturbed by the notion of *necromancy*. In actuality, consulting the dead is no different from consulting the living. Consult the ones you respect, those who are intelligent, wise and kind. If they respond, consider what they say with thought and care. Make your own decision, based on their advice and all other information available to you, and in accord with your values. Take responsibility for the outcomes of your choices.

Necromancy for Beginners

- *Ancestor Intensive*. This is very similar to the God/dess intensive exercise described in Chapter 5. Choose one of your personal Mighty Dead, perhaps one you identified and placed on your spiritual family tree. Research this person as thoroughly as you can. Read anything they wrote, along with any good biographies or commentaries on their work. If possible, visit places where they lived or worked. If that's not feasible, museums sometimes have rooms decorated in the styles of various periods. Find out what people ate, how they dressed, what music they listened to — any details you can about your chosen ancestor's time and place.

  Use this information to interact with your chosen ancestor. You might set up an altar, similar to a Mexican "Day of the Dead" altar, with their picture and things that would please them. Meditate there. You may be able to visit with your ancestor in your meditations. You can certainly write letters to them. You can also — in light meditation — write their responses. As usual, pay attention to your dreams and record your experience in your journal.

  If you're guiding a student through this exercise, ask them to do the research, and to bring a picture and/or other tokens of their chosen ancestor to a mentoring session. Then you can guide them in a meditative visit to their ancestor, using the trance techniques described in Chapter 5.

- *Dumb Supper*. Prepare a meal of your ancestor's favorite foods, or the foods that were typical of their time and place. Set the table nicely, including a full place setting for your ancestor. Put their picture or other token of their presence at their place setting. Formally invite their presence, perhaps by lighting a candle at their place setting, before you say grace. Say grace, then serve food to both yourself and your ancestor.

Eat in meditative silence. At the end of the meal, thank your ancestor for their company. Later, leave the food you offered to your ancestor outside, where it can return to earth.

A simpler variant is to pour two cups of tea or coffee or whatever your ancestor prefers. Drink one meditatively; later make a libation of the other.

For a group dumb supper, ask everyone to bring a small picture or token of their ancestor. Before the meal, go around the table and give each person a chance to introduce the guest they've brought. Say grace together. Eat in meditative silence.

- *The Feast of Samhain.* On November Eve, which is All Hallows Eve or Hallowe'en, Christians and Pagans alike ritually honor our Mighty Dead. We carve lanterns out of pumpkins to guide them to us. We toast their memories and praise their deeds. Believing the veil between our world and theirs to be thin on this night, we engage in all sorts of divination. We might have a dumb supper with them. Most of the year, we call them when we need their advice. This is the time when we throw a big party in their honor to thank them for all they did for us in life, and for all they still do.

MYTHOLOGY

One of the most important types of religious lore includes stories told about the God/desses. We call these stories myths. Myths are not facts, but neither are they lies or falsehoods. Here's how my *American Heritage Dictionary* defines the word *myth*:

A traditional, typically ancient, story dealing with supernatural beings, ancestors, or heroes that serves as a fundamental type in the world view of a people, as by explaining aspects of the natural world or delineating the psychology, customs, or ideals of society. A story, a theme, an object, or a character regarded as embodying an aspect of a culture. Such stories considered as a group.[2]

Some experiences, including that of Sacred Contact, are beyond words. They are ineffable, which means "incapable of being expressed; indescribable or unutterable."[3] What is ineffable cannot be told, only shown or shared. We share ineffable experiences, always imperfectly, through metaphor, symbol, ritual enactment, and myth. Myths are the great teaching stories told by the ancestors, polished through countless generations, conveying all that is strong and worthy in a culture.

Shared myths give us some sort of way to communicate about ineffable lived experience. If we share the cultural referents from which the myths are built, so much the better. Think of a graceful suspension bridge, poetry in form and function. The interaction of forces made visible by that construction is like the power of the Entheoi. The cultural referents are like the steel and stone and cable, materials with which we translate that power into visible and usable form. We compose our dreams from fragments of our day and our myths from fragments of our culture, but both tell us things we need to know.

Myths are also stories told by fallible human beings who are struggling to convey experiences beyond words. As people's consciousness is shaped, so the myths they create are shaped, by culture, gender, geography, class, and more. The proof of this is that myths demonstrably change over time, and vary from one place to another. If they were objective descriptions of literal facts, myths would be much more consistent across cultures and centuries, just as the chemical formula for water is the same everywhere.

The world was not created in six days flat. Aphrodite was not born of the ocean's spray. Not in the literal sense, although both those stories convey meaning and values within their native cultures, and maybe for others. It's important to discern what is deep mythic truth, and what is the cultural and personal overlay that masks and sometimes distorts it.

Think of myths as collective dreams, images that arise from the group mind rather than from the mind of the individual, structures of the cultural or subcultural egregore. Like dreams, these images and stories tell us much more than we thought we knew: they are the insights and wisdom of the deep mind, and perhaps the counsel of the Mighty Dead and the Entheoi. Also like dreams, the meanings of myths are not immediately obvious.

We can work with myths just as we work with dreams, exploring the threads of association and meaning that run through them. Because myths spring from a collective cultural unconscious rather than an individual or personal one, it's important to do some research first. This is essentially the same two-step process that I suggested for working with God/desses and ancestors. Study first, then meditate and dream.

Organizing material helps us to understand it. We can borrow two important organizational structures from scholarly, nonfundamentalist Christians:

- *Synoptic Gospels.* As you know, the Greek Bible contains four variant narratives of the life of Jesus, called the gospels. Three of these are very similar to each other. One way to present them, for the convenience of students, is in a three-column format, one narrative in each column. The gospels don't all cover the same incidents. When an episode is skipped in one of the gospels, blank space is left in that column, so the same stories appear side by side. This format allows readers to conveniently compare and contrast the reports of Matthew, Mark, and Luke.

For those myths that come from literate classical cultures, we also have a variety of tellings: Hesiod, Homer, and the Orphic hymns, for example. It might be possible to arrange some of them in parallel columns. At minimum, if you or your student is interested in a God/dess from a well-documented culture, you should read good translations of all the original source material you can, from different periods of that culture, paying careful attention to similarities and differences in the stories. See if you can relate those variations to invasions or migrations, changes in material culture, climate change, or change in any other aspect of that culture.

- *The Interpreter's Bible*. This reference work is intended as a resource for ministers preparing sermons, but the structure would be equally useful for any serious student of any mythic or liturgical text. It's really just a systematically and extremely annotated edition of the Bible. Each page is divided in three parts. The top section contains some of the Biblical text. The middle section holds scholarly notation: word origins, archeological notes, parallels with other contemporary myth systems — anything that seems interesting or relevant. The bottom section explores the application of the text to people's lives. The amount of space each section takes on any given page varies according to need.

Ask your students to use this method with any primary source material, ancient or modern. It will work just as well with sections of a good translation of the Mabinogion or the Egyptian Book of the Dead — or a poem by Doreen Valiente — as it does with the Bible.

In the middle section, write definitions of any unfamiliar words (tracing the word's roots can be really instructive), synopses of the stories of any God/desses mentioned, correspondences, notes about the cultural context of the selection. This is the scholarly part.

The bottom section traces inner connections. Write your personal associations and reflections. For very important concepts, consider adding a blank page and drawing a mind-map on it (see explanation later this chapter). Be alert to connections between the themes of the text and issues in your life.

Scholarship definitely comes first. But scholarship is simply a way of gathering all the ingredients. It's just a preparation for the real cooking. As with the God/dess and ancestor intensives, once the research is done, your student is ready for inner exploration. To do this, they must suspend disbelief, and act as if the myth were fact.

Skilled and experienced meditators may be able to shift consciousness alone. But it's difficult to have the full experience while maintaining enough separation to guide yourself. As a compromise, people can record their own trance guidance tapes, but that means the timing is pre-set and cannot be adjusted to the flow of the experience. Beginners do best to work with a guide or anchor — which usually means with their mentor.

Simply use the trance techniques described in Chapter 4 to take the student to that place in the Otherworld where the myth is eternally happening. The student may simply observe, or play a minor part, or actually assume the role of one of the God/desses, depending on their level of skill and confidence. Watch their reactions. Call them back if they seem to become too agitated, or wait for the scene to be completed. When they return, make sure they return fully. Remind them to pay attention to their dreams for the next few days and to record any insight, however it came to them, in their journal. Remind them also to follow through with any creative work that this experience may inspire.

Personal Mythology

Myths serve people as basic structures for interpreting our experiences, sources of power and guidance, vocabularies for communication about the inner worlds, doorways to Sacred Contact. They support the richness of spiritual life. But not always as well as they might.

We all inherit the myth system of our culture, and even more strongly, that of our immediate family. Only a very few of us were raised in Pagan households. Most adopted Paganism as a conscious, adult choice. We know, if anybody does, that inherited myths sometimes point us in ways we do not want to go.

Knowing this, and knowing that it is possible to choose, it makes little sense for us to abandon one mythic system only to adopt another whole cloth. Instead, we can take responsibility for creating our own personal synthesis from among all the teaching stories that are available to us. How? By magic, of course; by the sacred act of changing consciousness — and in this case, even changing the unconscious mind — in accordance with will.

There are many good books available with advice on specific techniques. I want to recommend one in particular: *The Mythic Path* by David Feinstein et al. (New York: Putnam, 1997), ISBN 0874778573. You can also get a tape containing the guided meditations from the book. It works as a self-guided system, but works even better when mentors who have worked through it themselves adapt the exercises to particular students' needs.

LEARNING METHODS

For my earlier book, *Wicca Covens*, I obtained catalogues from a sampling of Christian theological seminaries and compiled a list of their course requirements for their clergy preparation degree (usually an M.Div.). Then I asked a group of coven leaders what subjects they cover with students preparing for elder status. I was pleased to note that coven training includes most of the same subject matter as seminary training. Some subjects that were not covered are not relevant to coven work. The only glaring omission that I found in our training program was pedagogy. Nobody teaches Wiccan teachers how to teach![4] Of course, some of us were trained in teaching methods in secular life. I devoutly hope that somebody with that background will write a book on "Pedagogy for Pagans" very soon. Meanwhile, I want to share two of my favorite teaching techniques:

- *Mind-Map.* This exercise will help you trace the associative network around an idea, a God/dess, or even a person. Write the name or a short phrase identifying the idea in the center of a piece of unlined paper. Draw lines in any direction, and write associated ideas at the ends of those lines. Draw more branching lines from those ideas to others. If you perceive cross-links between branches, draw those lines too. The result will look like a spider web. Date the paper. Look at it again in a few days to see if you want to add to it. Think about what it shows you and write that in your journal. Save the mind map with your journal.
- *Brainstorms.* This exercise is for groups. Start with a concept and just have everybody call out ideas as they occur. Have somebody take notes. There is no censorship and no evaluation. By exploring a group's associative links, you can begin to get a feel for the group mind. Brainstorming is a good first step in problem solving or planning projects as well.

MORE AND MORE LORE

Of course, we inherit much more than myth from our ancestors. Each cumulative Tradition is likely to include

- rituals, which are often, but not always, enactments of myths;
- symbols: visual images, gestures, etc. that carry complex meaning;
- exercises and learning experiences;
- dances, chants, even rhythms;
- ethics and customs;
- curricula;
- explanations of how and why practices work; and
- notions of what to look for in a student, and of what constitutes "readiness" for entry into the group or advancement within it.

We've gone from notebooks to computer disks to hard drives full of such lore. We always had access to the collections of our own elders, but now the Internet allows us to draw from the collections of people we've never met. At the other extreme, some lore is still only transmitted orally. One way or another, we have far more than any one person or group can use. After a while, it's even hard for an individual to keep track of all the information they have on hand.

You have to pick. Every one of us has to create our own synthesis of this avalanche of lore, based on our own best understandings and values. And yet, if you are working within a structured Tradition, your choice is not entirely free. The heritage of lore allows us to share certain ineffable experiences, and these in turn sustain the precious sense of belongingness.

We need to find a harmonious and balanced interaction between the Entheos and the egregore — for the growth and the good of all.

TO LEARN MORE

McColman, Carl. *The Well-Read Witch*. Franklin Lakes: Career Press, 2002. ISBN 1564145301

Books of this nature are necessarily obsolete within three months of whenever the author submitted the manuscript. Still, this is an excellent snapshot of the good books available about Wicca and Paganism in 2001.

Metzger, Deena. *Writing For Your Life: a Guide and Companion to the Inner Worlds*. San Francisco: HarperSanFrancisco, 1992. ISBN 0062506129

Although this book is marketed to aspiring writers, it's really one of the finest books I know about spirituality. It contains great exercises for establishing relationships with spirits and God/desses. The section about contacting the spirits of writers you wish to emulate could be easily be applied to any of your Mighty Dead.

NOTES

[1] Miriam Benson, personal correspondence with author, 25 Dec. 2001.

[2] *American Heritage Dictionary*, 3rd ed. (electronic version)

[3] Ibid.

[4] Judy Harrow, *Wicca Covens* (Secaucus: Citadel, 1999), 154–56.

CONCLUSION
THE NEXT STRETCH

The road never ends. But it winds through the forest; often, we are unable to see very far ahead. It has rest stops and campsites. There's no rush to get anywhere. Beauty and knowledge are found all along the way.

Coming to the end of a book is like reaching a rest stop just before a bend in the ro ad. This is a good time to stop, reflect, maybe plan, perhaps take a guess at what adventures lie beyond those trees.

There's a little shop here. Is there anything we should pick up before continuing? What do Pagan spiritual mentors need?

I think we need more knowledge, but then I always want more knowledge. I think more networking, within and across Traditions, would be a wonderful help. Knowledge grows when we share it, as each of us can build on others' discoveries. As we learn together, as we rediscover our ancient path, questions may arise. Here are some that come up for me:

How can we best help people who face challenges we ourselves have not faced? Can we help people who are exploring practices we have not ourselves tried, or working with God/desses not known to us? How do we cope if a student seems to be surpassing our own achievements? What about another student who, under severe life stress, seems to be deteriorating?

I believe that the wisdom and power of the Entheoi shines through you. I hope that there will be many places for us to share our experiences and pool our knowledge. In a young religion, the elders must be each others' teachers.

May all your work be blessed! So mote it be.

APPENDIX A
GLOSSARY

Agape: Greek for unconditional and undemanding love. (p. 83)

Ancillary counseling: when a noncounseling professional such as a teacher, doctor, or clergy member helps a client work through emotional issues that come up in the course of their professional involvement. (p. 93)

And-gate: a situation in which two different things are needed before you can proceed, and neither will work without the other. "If we had ham, we could have ham and eggs . . . if we had eggs." (pp. 62, 111)

Anomie: literally "without norms," the condition of being without guiding values, without any basis for understanding which behaviors are right or wrong. (p. 107)

Asperge: consecrate space by sprinkling with water, or perhaps with an herbal infusion. (p. 86)

Authority: legitimation or validation for an action, belief, or status. "My skin, my bones, my heretic heart are my authority." — Catherine Madsen (pp. 24, 101, 125, 129, 131, 135, 142, 208, 209, 210)

Awen: Welsh word, usually translated as *poetic inspiration*. The real meaning is closer to *Sacred prophetic power*. Awen can overwhelm the unprepared recipient, throwing them into spiritual emergency. (pp. 54, 57, 62, 92, 108, 134, 136, 158, 161, 164, 166, 177, 199, 207, 221)

Cense: consecrate space with incense. If you are concerned about respiratory problems, use something like a feather fan to simply move the air. (p. 86)

Centering: concentration, inner focus, awareness of our boundaries and our deep selves. (pp. 169, 181, 187, 198)

Coach: to train or tutor or to act as a trainer or tutor. (pp. 71, 94, 174, 222–224) See *sponsor*.

Codependency: a fixation on solving other people's problems, thus both enabling them to continue in self-destructive behavior patterns and us to ignore our own problems and opportunities. Usually arises from an excessive need to be needed. Mentors, counselors, and clergy are at risk for codependency. (pp. 45, 58, 84, 85)

Congruence: the term comes from geometry, where it describes a condition in which two figures, when superimposed, match exactly. In psychology and religion, it means a similar matching of belief with behavior. Associated terms are *authenticity*, *genuineness*, and *integrity*. The magical equivalent of congruence is "acting in accordance," taking the practical actions that provide a channel for the power to manifest. In idiomatic usage, to be congruent is to "walk your talk." Note: congruent does not imply good. It's possible to live congruently with a belief system that is stupid, dysfunctional, or even evil. So the opposite of congruence is not evil; the opposite of congruence is hypocrisy. (pp. 14, 31, 115, 125, 136, 146, 149, 157, 158, 173, 178, 213, 214)

Counter-transference: a process whereby a mentor uses their relationship with a student to work out their own issues that arose elsewhere and usually in the past, instead of focusing on the student's current needs. (p. 136) See *transference*.

Cumulative tradition: the lore built up through a community's experience over the course of generations, and through reflection upon that experience. Each new generation uses this heritage to understand and integrate their own experience, then contributes to its further development. (pp. 135, 228, 241)

Dualism: the belief that the world is driven by two competing forces, usually understood to be good and evil. (p. 105)

Egregore: the group mind of a magical or spiritual group, built up through many shared explorations of the inner planes. Initiation is believed to give the new member access to a group's egregore. (pp. 219, 220, 233, 237)

Empathy: the ability to share another person's perceptual field and emotional responses, to understand deeply how it is for them. (pp. 43, 72, 73, 74, 76, 77, 78, 79, 85, 161)

Energy: magical power raised and directed towards a goal. Other cultures have other terms for this, such as *mana, orenda,* or *prana.* (pp. 65, 140, 147, 157, 158)

Entheoi: the indwelling Gods; plural form of entheos. (pp. 29, 30, 31, 32, 46, 54, 62, 72, 73, 74, 84, 85, 87, 89, 95, 125, 136, 157, 158, 160, 161, 163, 166, 172, 173, 174, 199, 207, 210, 223, 232, 236, 237, 245)

Entheos: Greek for the indwelling God. (pp. 27, 242)

Epiphany: a moment of revelation; a sudden and intuitive realization of the essence and meaning of something, often of Deity, that brings about new perception or comprehension of its real nature. (pp. 123, 163, 173) See *gnosis, sacrament.*

Esoteric: inner, hidden, mystical aspects of a religion (opposite of *exoteric*). (pp. 48, 55, 103, 112)

Ethics: a set of rules for living derived from core values and social consensus. (pp. 33, 38, 39, 43, 49, 54, 58, 80, 81, 129, 131, 134, 136, 143, 207–213, 242)

Exoteric: outer, public, conventional aspects of a religion (opposite of *esoteric*). (pp. 48, 103, 112, 134)

Faith: a trusting, loving relationship with Deity that forms the basis and the model for all our life commitments. (pp. 125, 126–136)

Fundamentalism: originally a retrogressive movement of American Protestants who opposed the widespread adoption of Darwin's theory of evolution. This movement to restore belief in literal Biblical inerrancy took the name *fundamentalist* in 1920. The term has since generalized to include similar movements in other religions; for example, the Taliban who, until recently, imposed an extreme and repressive version of Islamic rule in Afghanistan. Fundamentalists typically believe that their way is the one, true, right, and only way to relate to Deity or conduct one's life. Fundamentalist tendencies afflict every religion. (pp. 23, 125, 147, 214)

Generativity: in psychologist Erik Erikson's theory of stages in adult psycho-social development, generativity is the term for mature adults' need to influence the future by working with the young. This need can be addressed by raising children, teaching school, mentoring younger colleagues, etc. (pp. 62, 103, 104, 107, 111, 221)

Gnosis: primary, intuitive, or experiential apprehension of spiritual truths. Sudden integration of understanding and/or transformation of consciousness. Knowledge derived from epiphany, rather than from research or reasoning. Knowledge that can be shared but cannot be told. (p. 173) See also *epiphany, mystery, sacrament.*

Grace: in theology, Divine love and protection freely bestowed; undeserved gifts. (pp. 28, 30, 31)

Grounding: (1) connection with the earth/ground; creating a cyclical current of pulling up, running through, and releasing excess awen that, ideally, is constantly in motion. Maintaining the flow protects us from draining our individual reserves. ("Be a faucet, not a pitcher.") (2) releasing excess awen so we can return to an ordinary and safe state of consciousness. Although *grounding* is the traditional term for both connection and release, we can draw awen from or release excess awen to any of the four elements, or even blend them. Primary reliance on the element Earth is most appropriate for Earth religion, but not absolutely required. (pp. 71, 78, 87, 165, 169, 181, 187, 195, 198)

Henotheism: devotion to one God (or perhaps two) while respectfully recognizing the existence of many others. (p. 26)

Holding environment: the helping relationship understood as a safe space from which the client can explore new ways of thinking and acting. Comparable to the ritual Circle. (pp. 83–88, 195)

Ideal type: a way of being or behaving which, while impossible to perfectly achieve, is held out as a standard or model of perfection or excellence. A source of guidance; a goal towards which we can and should aspire. (pp. 127, 128) (*navigational star*, pp. 149–50)

Idealizing transference: a form of transference in which one's ideals and aspirations are projected onto another, such as a therapist or mentor. This creates a visible goal, and thus allows us to believe that our aspirations are achievable. (pp. 44–46)

Immanence: the theological model in which the Sacred dwells within the manifest world, within ourselves and one another. (pp. 26, 27)

Impostor syndrome: the fear that I don't really know what I'm doing, that I'm only faking it and will soon be caught. Often this is a goad to ongoing learning and growth in skill. Impostor syndrome often afflicts the best workers in any field, including mentoring. (pp. 41, 45)

Ineffable: incapable of being expressed; indescribable or unutterable. (pp. 169, 170, 236) See *mystery*.

Inner plane: the personal unconscious, the egregore of a particular group, the general collective unconscious that all humans share, and perhaps the Otherworld, which is the realm of the Gods. In a panentheistic model, the Otherworld includes, but is not limited to, the various levels of human unconscious. (p. 98, 133, 187)

Inscape: a person's inner world, their perceptions, reactions, memories, hopes, fears, and dreams. (pp. 72, 74, 77, 78)

Karma: an imported Sanskrit word originally describing a Hindu concept. As used in Paganism, it simply means the logical outcomes of our actions, the ultimately fair process of cause and effect. "What goes around comes around." Those who believe in reincarnation usually also believe that unresolved karma can play out over the course of many lifetimes. (pp. 134, 141)

Magic: (1) the art of changing consciousness in accordance with will. (2) the art of causing change in accordance with will. (pp. 58, 72, 85, 86, 105, 141, 161, 170, 180, 240)

Meditation: a variety of methods for stilling the rational mind, calming surface distractions, and focusing on inner wisdom. (pp. 120, 139, 146, 151, 164, 175, 180, 183, 187, 222, 234)

Metaphor: one thing conceived as representing another. (pp. 26, 54, 57, 83, 125, 129, 131, 135, 150, 158, 167, 170, 188, 195, 225, 236)

Mighty Dead: chosen ancestors of the spirit. Historical figures whose lives instruct and inspire us, whether or not they are actual blood kin; saints. (pp. 38, 85, 128, 231–235, 237)

Model: (1) model *of*: a schematic description of an object, relationship, or theory that accounts for its known or inferred properties and can be used for further study of its characteristics. (2) model *for*: an example to be imitated or compared; for example, a dress pattern or a blueprint. So religion offers both a model *of* the Sacred and a model *for* congruent living, thus connecting belief and behavior. (pp. 23, 24, 25, 31, 33, 35, 56, 58, 76, 77, 78, 97, 102, 104, 105, 106, 107, 108, 109, 110, 111, 112, 113, 114, 116, 119, 121, 126, 127, 128, 141, 158, 159, 168, 170, 190, 193, 222, 232)

Mystery: something that cannot be fully explained in words, but must be grasped by direct experience. Knowledge that can be shared but cannot be told. When capitalized, Mystery refers specifically to the experience of Sacred Presence, but it can also mean baking bread, listening to music, making love. (pp. 125, 167, 229) See *gnosis*.

Mysticism: the quest for a closer experiential relationship with Deity. (pp. 27, 28, 31, 42, 48, 49, 56, 66, 112, 113, 115, 158, 159, 163, 186, 188, 189, 191, 199)

Myth: a traditional and typically ancient story dealing with supernatural beings, ancestors, or heroes that serves as a fundamental type in the worldview of a people by explaining aspects of the natural world or delineating the psychology, customs, or ideals of society. A story, a theme, an object, or a character regarded as embodying an aspect of a culture. Such stories considered as a group. Myths need not be literally true; they carry meanings and values, not facts. (pp. 17, 22, 25, 183, 235–240)

Necromancy: the practice of communicating with the spirits of the dead. (pp. 233–235)

Ordinary reality: the World of Form, the manifest world, opposite of the Otherworld. (pp. 53, 55, 172, 182, 184, 189, 190, 192) (also *ordinary consciousness*)

Otherworld: the realm of the Gods, of unmanifest potential, counterpart to the world of form. (pp. 135, 180, 183, 184, 187, 189, 190, 192, 196, 197, 198, 232, 239)

Panentheism: a theological orientation that perceives the Sacred as both pervading and transcending the manifest universe. (pp. 27, 29, 31, 112, 141, 166)

Pantheism: a theological orientation that identifies Deity with the manifest universe; closely related to the concept of immanence. (p. 27)

Paradigm: a "master story," a meaning system. The central organizing pattern for any area of inquiry or thought. (p. 125)

Peak experience: mystical experience, moment of perception of the Sacred beauty and power within which we live. (pp. 159–160, 166, 172–174)

Polarity: a situation in which two principles are both considered desirable, but are understood as being opposite or reciprocal to one another, so more of one means less of the other. Polarities do not challenge us to choose; they challenge us to balance, to go for both/and. We get into difficulties when we become unbalanced. (pp. 106, 107, 147, 212)

Power of naming: an important method of changing consciousness in accordance with will. (p. 105) See *magic*; see also *Sapir-Whorf hypothesis*.

Reframing: redefining an experience to give it new and more beneficial meaning. For example, accidentally getting lost in the woods in the dark can be reframed as an initiatory challenge. This is an application of the magical power of naming. (pp. 65, 115)

Sacrament: experiential evidence of Sacred Presence. A sacrament may induce an epiphany. (pp. 28, 29, 31, 32)

Sapir-Whorf hypothesis: the proposition that the language we use deeply influences the way we think, generally credited to Edward Sapir (1884–1939) and Benjamin Lee Whorf (1897–1941). (pp. 105, 113)

Scrying: gazing at an object or surface using a relaxed, meditative, "soft-eyed" gaze, allowing images to arise from the deep mind. Conscious and intentional projection, free of the problems that arise from unconscious projection onto people and things in daily life. Scryers may use the stereotypical crystal ball, but many other, less expensive objects work just as well: a black mirror, a bowl of water, ink blots, clouds. (p. 130)

Shaman: one who trances, dreams, or otherwise explores the Otherworld on behalf of the community or tribe; a "technician of the Sacred." Although the word itself is Siberian, similar specialists exist in many indigenous cultures all over the world. Contemporary Wicca is our loving reconstruction of European shamanism, after centuries of persecution and neglect. (pp. 54, 148–149, 162, 165, 190, 191, 192, 196, 197, 198)

Sign: an item or action that communicates a single, simple meaning (e.g., a traffic sign). Not complex or multivocal like a symbol. (pp. 28, 131, 182)

Spiritual emergency (or spiritual emergence): a crisis that occurs when a person who is actively engaged in some meditative or spiritual practice becomes overwhelmed by the intensity of the experiences they achieve, and may be temporarily unable to function in a normal manner. (pp. 49, 54, 86, 115, 121, 130, 149, 166, 188–199)

Spirituality: conscious contact with the Sacred; activities intended to create, maintain, clarify, deepen, or increase Sacred Contact. (pp. 13, 26, 32, 39, 40, 46, 53, 58, 121, 146, 147, 156, 207, 229)

Sponsor: a person who vouches for another person's suitability for a position. A person who assumes responsibility for another person or a group during a period of instruction, apprenticeship, or probation. (pp. 224–225) See *coach.*

Symbol: an item or action that carries associations or connotations of something else, often something invisible; a token; a visible or tangible metaphor. Symbols are complex and multivocal in contrast to simple signs. (pp. 13, 49, 135, 197, 236, 242)

Transcendence: the theological model in which the Sacred is radically separated from the manifest world (Holy wholly other). (pp. 26, 28)

Transference: the process by which emotions and desires originally associated with someone in our past, usually a family member, are unconsciously shifted to someone in our present, possibly a mentor. When a mentor projects their own prior experience onto a student, it is called *counter-transference*. (p. 44)

Turing test: a computer passes the Turing test if it can simulate human responses to the point where an impartial judge, asking questions of both the computer and a human, cannot determine which is which. (p. 233)

Unitive experience: a peak experience that involves a perception of unity with some good greater than ourselves, such as nature, the universe, or Deity. (p. 30)

Values: guiding principles, derived from the Latin *valere*, which means *strong* or *worthy*. (pp. 39, 40, 45, 47, 49, 71, 112, 143, 173, 207, 213–217, 237)

Wiccan Rede: the central ethic of Wicca, generally applicable to a Pagan way of life. The Rede teaches personal autonomy tempered by respect for others:

Eight words the Wiccan Rede fulfill:

An it harm none, do what you will!

(pp. 33, 82, 106, 212) [Note: *rede* is an archaic term meaning *advice*; *an* is an archaic term meaning *if*.]

Will: a personal sense of purpose, deliberate intention, determination, self-responsibility. (pp. 29, 31, 32, 57, 58, 86, 142, 143, 147, 161, 170, 214)

World of Form: the manifest world, ordinary or consensus reality, counterpart to the Otherworld. (pp. 26, 53, 55, 192, 198, 214)

APPENDIX B
COUNCIL ON SPIRITUAL PRACTICES: CODE OF ETHICS FOR SPIRITUAL GUIDES

[Preamble]

People have long sought to enrich their lives and to awaken to their full natures through spiritual practices including prayer, meditation, mind-body disciplines, service, ritual, community liturgy, holy-day and seasonal observances, and rites of passage. "Primary religious practices" are those intended, or especially likely, to bring about exceptional states of consciousness such as the direct experience of the divine, of cosmic unity, or of boundless awareness.

In any community, there are some who feel called to assist others along spiritual paths, and who are known as ministers, rabbis, pastors, curanderas, shamans, priests, or other titles. We call such people "guides": those experienced in some practice, familiar with the terrain, and who act to facilitate the spiritual practices of others. A guide need not claim exclusive or definitive knowledge of the terrain.

Spiritual practices, and especially primary religious practices, carry risks. Therefore, when an individual chooses to practice with the assistance of a guide, both take on special responsibilities. The Council on Spiritual Practices proposes the following Code of Ethics for those who serve as spiritual guides.

1. [Intention] Spiritual guides are to practice and serve in ways that cultivate awareness, empathy, and wisdom.

2. [Serving Society] Spiritual practices are to be designed and conducted in ways that respect the common good, with due regard for public safety, health, and order. Because the increased awareness gained from spiritual practices can catalyze desire for personal and social change, guides shall use special care to help direct the energies of those they serve, as well as their own, in responsible ways that reflect a loving regard for all life.

3. [Serving Individuals] Spiritual guides shall respect and seek to preserve the autonomy and dignity of each person. Participation in any primary religious practice must be voluntary and based on prior disclosure and consent given individually by each participant while in an ordinary state of consciousness. Disclosure shall include, at a minimum, discussion of any elements of the practice that could reasonably be seen as presenting physical or psychological risks. In particular, participants must be warned that primary religious experience can be difficult and dramatically transformative.

Guides shall make reasonable preparations to protect each participant's health and safety during spiritual practices and in the periods of vulnerability that may follow. Limits on the behaviors of participants and facilitators are to be made clear and agreed upon in advance of any session. Appropriate customs of confidentiality are to be established and honored.

4. [Competence] Spiritual guides shall assist with only those practices for which they are qualified by personal experience and by training or education.

5. [Integrity] Spiritual guides shall strive to be aware of how their own belief systems, values, needs, and limitations affect their work. During primary religious practices, participants may be especially open to suggestion, manipulation, and exploitation;

therefore, guides pledge to protect participants and not to allow anyone to use that vulnerability in ways that harm participants or others.

6. [Quiet Presence] To help safeguard against the harmful consequences of personal and organizational ambition, spiritual communities are usually better allowed to grow through attraction rather than active promotion.

7. [Not for Profit] Spiritual practices are to be conducted in the spirit of service. Spiritual guides shall strive to accommodate participants without regard to their ability to pay or make donations.

8. [Tolerance] Spiritual guides shall practice openness and respect towards people whose beliefs are in apparent contradiction to their own.

9. [Peer Review] Each guide shall seek the counsel of other guides to help ensure the wholesomeness of his or her practices and shall offer counsel when there is need.

This draft for public comment was released 10 August 2001. The current version is available on the Internet at <www.csp.org>.

Copyright © 1995–2001
Council on Spiritual Practices
Box 460820
San Francisco, CA 94146-0820
USA

Permission is hereby given to reprint this Code, provided that the text is reproduced complete and verbatim, including the CSP contact information, copyright, and this notice of limited permission to reprint.

<www.csp.org/development/code.html>

INDEX

We shall not cease from exploration
And the end of all our exploring
Will be to arrive where we started
And know the place for the first time.

— T.S. Eliot, *The Four Quartets*